The Art of
Japanese Architecture

David and Michiko Young

Photography by
David and Michiko Young
Ben Simmons
Keyphotos
Murata Noboru

Illustrations by
Tan Hong Yew

TUTTLE PUBLISHING
Tokyo • Rutland, Vermont • Singapore

Published by Tuttle Publishing, an imprint of
Periplus Editions (HK) Ltd., with editorial offices at
364 Innovation Drive, North Clarendon, Vermont
05759 U.S.A, and 130 Joo Seng Road #06-01,
Singapore 368357.

Library of Congress Control Number
2006929874

ISBN-13: 978 0 8048 3838 2
ISBN-10: 0 8048 3838 0
Printed in Singapore

Distributed by:
North America, Latin America and Europe
Tuttle Publishing, 364 Innovation Drive,
North Clarendon, Vermont 05759, USA.
Tel: (802) 773 8930; Fax: (802) 773 6993
E-mail: info@tuttlepublishing.com
http://www.tuttlepublishing.com

Japan
Tuttle Publishing, Yaekari Building, 3F,
5-4-12 Osaki, Shinagawa-ku, Tokyo 141-0032.
Tel: (813) 5437 0171; Fax: (813) 5437 0755
Email: tuttle-sales@gol.com

Asia Pacific
Berkeley Books Pte Ltd, 130 Joo Seng Road
#06-01, Singapore 368357.
Tel: (65) 6280 1330; Fax: (65) 6280 6290
E-mail: inquiries@periplus.com.sg
http://www.periplus.com

09 08 07
6 5 4 3 2 1

**Front endpaper: Teahouse and Zen garden at
Jomyōji Temple, Kamakura.**
Back endpaper: Tokyo from Roppongi Hills Tower.
**Page 1: Ceremonial gate to the 1894 Satō
country house, Oomagari City, Akita Prefecture.**
**Page 2: Interior décor in the 70-year-old home
of tea aficionado Satō Teizō, Osaka.**
Pages 4–5: Interior of Ryōanji Temple.
Page 6: Great Hall of Tōdaiji Temple (page 40).
Pages 8–9: Eiheiji Temple in autumn (page 97).

Contents

Traditional Japanese Architecture: An Overview

Japanese traditional architecture can be organized into several major genealogical groups on the basis of historical origins and stylistic influences. The most important group is composed primarily of palace, residential, and teahouse styles originating in prehistoric raised structures. Other major groups are commoner residences that evolved from prehistoric pit structures, Buddhist temples, Shinto shrines, theaters, and castles. The diagram below has been simplified to emphasize major trends.

HISTORICAL PERIODS

JŌMON
10000–300 BCE

YAYOI
300 BCE–300 CE

TOMB MOUND
300–710 (overlaps with later periods)

ASUKA
538–645

HAKUHŌ
645–710

NARA
710–794

HEIAN
794–1185

KAMAKURA
1185–1333

MUROMACHI
1333–1573

MOMOYAMA
1573–1600

EDO
1600–1868

MEIJI
1868–1912

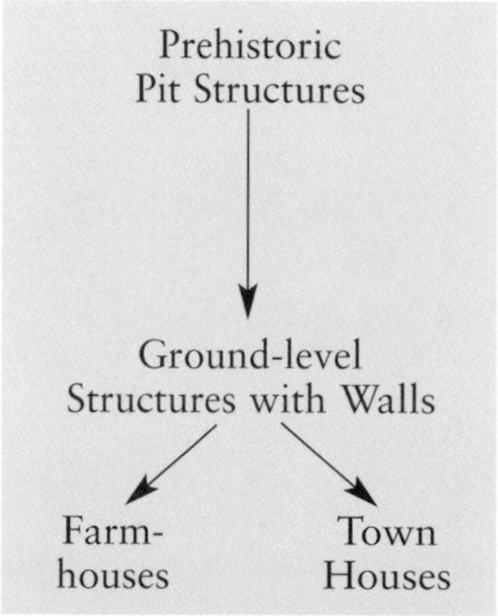

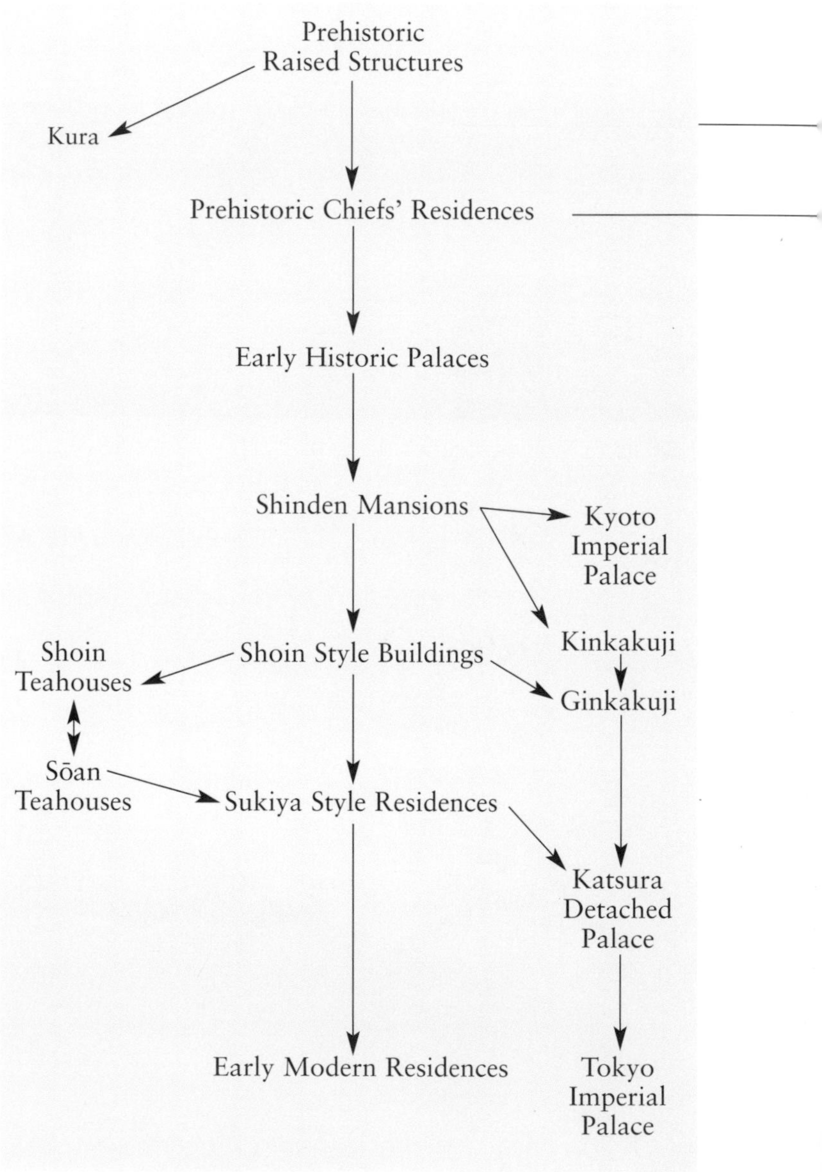

Kinkakuji Temple, Kyoto.

Reception room, Zanyūsō house.

Prehistoric Pit Structures → Ground-level Structures with Walls → Farmhouses / Town Houses

Prehistoric Raised Structures → Kura / Prehistoric Chiefs' Residences → Early Historic Palaces → Shinden Mansions → Kyoto Imperial Palace / Kinkakuji

Shinden Mansions → Shoin Style Buildings → Shoin Teahouses / Kinkakuji / Ginkakuji

Shoin Teahouses ↕ Sōan Teahouses → Sukiya Style Residences

Sukiya Style Residences → Katsura Detached Palace → Tokyo Imperial Palace / Early Modern Residences

Yasaka Shrine, Kyoto.

Jōruriji Temple, Nara.

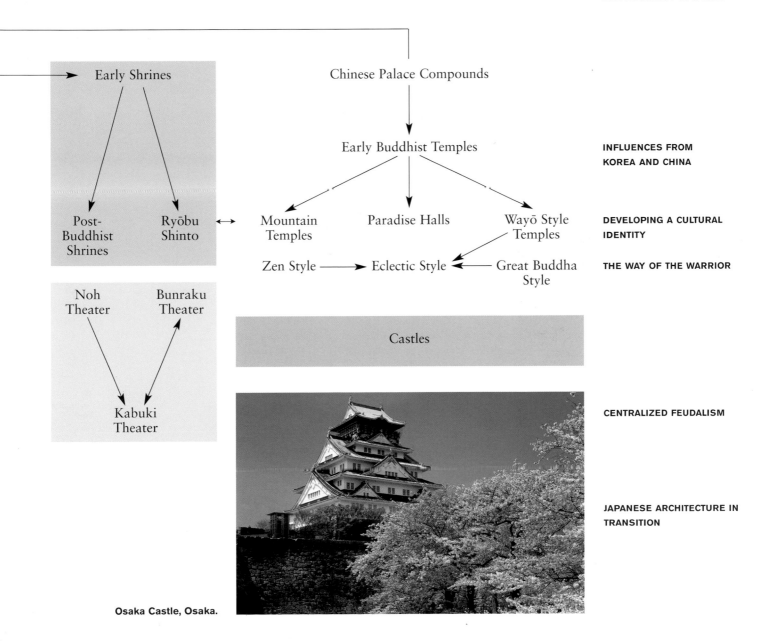

Early Shrines

Chinese Palace Compounds

Early Buddhist Temples

Post-Buddhist Shrines   Ryōbu Shinto

Mountain Temples   Paradise Halls   Wayō Style Temples

Zen Style ⟶ Eclectic Style ⟵ Great Buddha Style

Noh Theater   Bunraku Theater

Kabuki Theater

Castles

Osaka Castle, Osaka.

Basic Principles

Many architectural styles have developed over the course of Japan's long history. Nevertheless, there are several basic principles that can be found in the interesting but complex story told in the following pages. Some of these basic principles describe how core values have influenced the choice of building materials, techniques, and designs. Other principles emphasize cultural processes such as the relation between restraint and exuberance and a passion for preserving the past.

Above: The Japanese love of wood is illustrated in the Zenshitsu Hall at Gangōji Temple in Nara City.

Opposite: The entrance to the 100-year-old Nakamura house in Wajima City, which faces the Japan Sea at the northern end of the Noto Peninsula, has been waterproofed and protected from decay by 20–30 coats of lacquer (*urushi*), a long tradition in an area known for its lacquer guilds and refined lacquerware.

Natural Materials and Settings

Traditional Japanese architecture is characterized by a preference for natural materials, in particular wood. Since wood can breathe, it is suitable for the Japanese climate. Wood absorbs humidity in the wet months and releases moisture when the air is dry. With proper care and periodic repairs, traditional post-and-beam structures can last as long as 1,000 years. Other natural building materials are reeds, bark, and clay used for roofing, and stones used for supporting pillars, surfacing building platforms, and holding down board roofs, with an emphasis upon straight lines, asymmetry, simplicity of design, and understatement, exemplified by pre-Buddhist Shinto shrines, farmhouses, teahouses, and tasteful contemporary interiors.

There is also a distinct preference for natural settings. After Buddhism was introduced to Japan from the continent, it was not long before the symmetry of Chinese temple compounds gave way to mountain temples with an asymmetrical layout.

Restraint and Exuberance

There is, however, another side to Japanese culture that is not as well known – the appreciation of exuberant colors and complexity of form – in contrast to the restrained tradition with its simplicity and asymmetry. This is exemplified by Chinese style shrines and

temples and the mausoleums at Nikkō. Such buildings are characterized by a strong contrast between vermilion posts and white plastered walls, elaborate decorations, curved lines, symmetry, and the imposition of order upon nature. Both the restrained and exuberant traditions are favored at different times and places, depending upon the occasion. For example, ceremonial buildings are designed to impress and thus tend to be more exuberant than residential architecture, where the goal is to provide a tasteful and relaxed atmosphere for the occupants.

Attention to Detail

Regardless of whether circumstances call for restraint or exuberance, Japanese architects, builders, artists, and craftspeople pay a great deal of attention to detail. Even when the overall effect of a building is simple, particularly when it is viewed from a distance, a close-up inspection of the building often reveals numerous details that add interest. Attention to detail applies to both technological and design features. For example, at the technological level, the intricate joinery of a traditional building allowed it to be assembled without nails and to be disassembled periodically for repairs. At the design level, the interlocking eave supports of a Buddhist temple can be quite complicated. The basic pattern of the brackets, however, is repeated over and over again to create a visual rhythm that is well integrated and unified.

Indigenous and Foreign Influences

Japanese society has been inundated at various times by cultural influences from abroad. In early times, these influences came primarily from Korea and China; more recently, mostly from Europe and the United States. In both cases, the Japanese welcomed foreign influences and attempted to copy what were perceived to be superior cultures. A reaction eventually set in, with the result that foreign influences were assimilated and made part of the Japanese tradition. Rather than being overwhelmed by foreign cultures, the Japanese

Right: The wood carving on the bottom of the door, as well as the metalwork which graces an adjacent pillar, both part of a gate at Higashi Honganji Temple in Kyoto, illustrate the attention to detail that is typical of many traditional buildings.

repeatedly have demonstrated a talent for creatively blending different influences into new styles that express basic Japanese values and aesthetic preferences.

Preserving the Past

Considerable effort is expended upon preserving old buildings. This requires dealing with the advantages and disadvantages of wood, the most popular building material in traditional Japan. Wood is easy to work with, it can be fashioned into a variety of shapes, and it can be used to create structures that are earthquake resistant. The main disadvantage

of wood is that it rots and burns. The Japanese have dealt with this disadvantage in a number of ways.

Regular renewal involves the custom, associated with early Shinto shrines, of periodically making a more or less exact copy of a building, after which the original is torn down. The most famous example of regular renewal is Ise Jingū, the most important of the early imperial shrines. Regular renewal made it unnecessary to be overly concerned about decay since even posts planted directly in the ground, a method used in early shrines, usually survive until a building is dismantled and a new one built.

Above: The majestic two-story Satō country house, viewed through slats in the perimeter wall, has a heavy roof, deep overhangs, and wood-wrapped walls designed to withstand extreme weather conditions.

Opposite: The relationship between the interior and the garden is very important in Sukiya style architecture, here mediated by the wood-floored *engawa* corridor.

Above: The Main Hall and Meditation Hall at Gangōji Temple. These beautiful multi-colored tiles, made by Korean craftsmen in the Asuka Period, are the oldest tiles in Japan. The more recent tiles used on the adjacent roof slope to the right are more uniform in color.

Above: This close-up of a post at Hōryūji Temple, near Nara, demonstrates one method of preservation: cutting out a rotted piece of wood and replacing it with a plug made from the same kind of material.

Opposite: The Kusakabe family, merchants and financiers in the Edo Period, rebuilt their mansion after an 1879 fire. The interior is dominated by massive posts and beams that support a high ceiling. Despite its grandeur, the overall effect is simple and dignified.

Right: Reconstruction of the Main Hall at Yakushiji Temple in Nara was completed in 1976, after being destroyed centuries earlier, on the basis of archaeological evidence, a Heian Period document, and a surviving pagoda on the grounds.

A common practice in traditional Japan was to *recycle* materials, such as using lumber and tiles from buildings that have collapsed, been partially destroyed by fire or war, or intentionally torn down, in the construction or repair of other buildings. For example, tile was invented in China about 4,000 years ago, but old tiles apparently were not reused. In Japan, however, tiles frequently were salvaged from dismantled buildings and used in the construction of new buildings – often in connection with the frequent moves of the early capitals.

Preservation is the practice of taking steps to save architectural members that are decaying, and reinforcing structures that are in danger of collapse. For example, the five-story pagoda at Honmonji Temple in Tokyo was built in 1608. After 400 years, the pagoda had developed a number of serious problems. Eaves brackets were being crushed from the weight of the roof and the bottom portion of many of the posts on the first level were rotten. Normally all of these parts would be replaced. Because of the fear that the building would lose its cultural value if this were done, however, the damaged parts were injected with carbon fiber. In this way, 70 percent of the damaged parts were preserved.

In contrast to preservation, *remodeling* involves modifying a structure to bring it into line with contemporary styles or to enable it to meet the requirements of a revised function. One of the most interesting examples of remodeling is the Higashi Chōshūden, a building constructed in the early eighth century (Nara Period) for government workers at the Heijōkyō palace. The building was remodeled as a temple around 760 when it was moved to become the Lecture Hall of Tōshōdaiji Temple in Nara. In the process of remodeling, the slope of the roof was increased and its shape was altered. In addition, the bays between the posts were filled in with walls, doors, and windows to make it resemble other temples from that period. The Lecture Hall was remodeled again in the thirteenth century, giving its current appearance.

In *restoration*, those parts of a structure that have been damaged by natural forces, such as fire, or that have decayed over time and cannot be saved, are replaced. To continue the story of Tōshōdaiji Temple related above, when it was decided in the year 2000 that the Main Hall had to undergo a major restoration, a one-tenth scale model was constructed and exact measurements were taken of every part of the building. The hall's main frame consists of 20,000 interlocking parts that fit together like a giant jigsaw puzzle, without the use of nails, making it possible to take the building apart without serious damage. Each piece of wood that is being removed is given a tag indicating its original location, and is replicated if necessary.

Frequently, there is nothing left to be preserved, remodeled, or restored. *Reconstruction* refers to the necessity of rebuilding a structure that no longer exists, or replacing parts of a structure that have been lost. For example, in 1967 Yakushiji Temple in Nara embarked upon a large-scale program of reconstructing the grandeur of its original Nara Period compound. The first project was to restore the Main Hall that had been destroyed several centuries earlier. There were no extant drawings, but fortunately the temple possessed a Heian Period document that described the original temple complex. On the basis of this and other evidence, such as an archaeological excavation of the original site, the Main Hall was back in its original position in 1976, after nine years of intensive effort.

Status and Function

For many centuries Japan has been a hierarchical society, with considerable emphasis upon status, authority, and power. Differences in architectural styles provide a material expression of these differences in rank. To some extent, the history of Japanese traditional architecture can be viewed in terms of the contrast between the architecture of the élite and the architecture of common people. The former is exemplified by palaces and villas, as well as the temples and shrines patronized by rulers. The latter can be seen in farmhouses and the shop-dwellings of merchants. These

élite and commoner traditions are, however, not immutable. They sometimes come together, as in the case of a wealthy farmer who includes a formal Shoin style room, associated with élite dwellings, in his farmhouse.

Differences in architectural styles are also associated with differences in function. Thus the styles of a Shinto shrine and Buddhist temple can be quite distinct, despite the fact that they both are religious edifices. Here again, however, the differences should not be over-emphasized. Shinto and Buddhist architecture often influenced each other, and at one time the two religions were even combined, creating an eclectic style of religious architecture.

The structure that most concretely indicates status and function is the *gate*. Gates have practical significance in terms of controlling access to spaces. They also have symbolic significance in that their design, size, and materials indicate something about the wealth and power of their owners or the people who enter. A few examples are described below.

A *torii* is a gate without doors that marks the entrance to a Shinto shrine precinct. Literally, *torii* means "where the birds are." Some scholars have suggested that originally *torii* may have provided a perch for sacred birds, such as the chickens which played a role in a famous myth about the sun goddess, the ancestress of the imperial line. Regardless of the origins of *torii*, their main function is to provide a dividing line between the exterior profane world and the interior sacred space where the *kami* dwell (see pages 30–1). *Torii* are constructed of wood, stone, or metal and are sometimes painted red. They vary in size from small structures, such as those at the entrance to a neighborhood shrine, to enormous edifices that mark the entry to a major Shinto compound. After the coming of Buddhism, many major shrines adopted a Buddhist style gate, retaining one or more *torii* to mark the approach.

Early temples in Japan were based on the Chinese custom of enclosing important buildings in a fenced compound with a gate on the south. There are three basic types of temple gates. The first, a single-story gate, can be constructed in different sizes and can vary considerably in terms of the complexity of the decorations. For example, a *karamon* is a relatively small single-story gate with a curved Chinese style roof and ornate decorations. The second, a *rōmon* is a two-story gate with

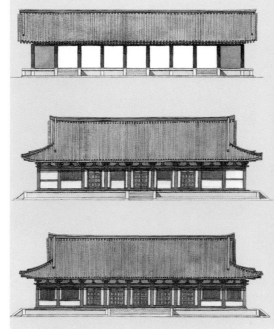

Examples of Remodeling
The Lecture Hall at Tōshōdaiji Temple in Nara underwent a move and was successively remodeled.

Top: A model of the eighth-century Higashi Chōshūden (government workers' building), at the Heijōkō palace. The model is located at the Heijō Palace Site Museum in Nara.

Middle: A model of Higashi Chōshūden after it was moved to Tōshōdaiji Temple in the eighth century and remodeled as the Lecture Hall. The model is located at the Heijō Palace Site Museum in Nara.

Bottom: The Lecture Hall as it appears today.

a single roof. Thirdly, a *nijūmon* is a two-story structure with a double roof. *Rōmon* and *nijūmon* often have guardian deities in alcoves on both sides of the entrance. *Nijūmon* originally were used in large Nara Period temple complexes such as Tōdaiji and Yakushiji, but are also typical of later Jōdo and Zen temples and monasteries. The *rōmon*, used in both temples and many major post-Buddhist shrines, was an adaptation of the *nijūmon* in which the roof above the first floor was replaced by a simple balcony. The choice of which gate to use depended upon the status and function of the temple.

A good example of the use of gates to symbolize power is the samurai gate. The third Tokugawa shogun, Iemitsu, required that all *daimyo* scheduled to receive an official shogunal visit (*onari*) at their Edo residence must prepare for the occasion by building special facilities, the most important of which was an elaborate gate known as *onarimon*.

None of these Edo *onarimon* have survived, but the style is exemplified by the *karamon* of Nishi Honganji Temple in Kyoto. Originally an imperial messenger gate at Hideyoshi's Momoyama castle at Fushimi, the gate was moved to Nishi Honganji when Hideyoshi's castle was dismantled. It was rebuilt for a visit by Iemitsu in 1632. The

Opposite: Tōji Temple (page 54).

Above: There is no set design for garden gates and they can be made with a variety of materials.

Temple and Shrine Gates

The importance of a temple or shrine is often indicated by the size and complexity of its gate(s), of which there are three basic types: single-story gates, two-story gates with a single roof, and two-story gates with a double roof.

Right: *Munemon*: two posts, one story, e.g. Enshōji Temple, Nara Prefecture.

Far right: *Shikyakumon*: four posts, one story, e.g. Enryakuji Temple, Shiga Prefecture.

Right: *Yatsuashimon*: eight posts, one story, e.g. Ishiya-madera Temple, Shiga Prefecture.

Far right: *Rōmon*: eight or twelve posts, two stories, one roof, e.g. Tōdaiji Temple, Nara City.

Right: *Nijūmon*: eight or twelve posts, two stories, two roofs, e.g. Chionin Temple, Kyoto City.

Far right: The entrance to the compounds of most major Shinto shrines consists of a Buddhist style gate, e.g. Heian Shrine, Kyoto City.

emperor followed a similar custom. When he scheduled a visit to a temple or palace, or sent a delegate on his behalf, special facilities, including an imperial gate, had to be prepared.

Shrine, temple, and samurai gates are largely symbolic, in contrast to castle gates, which had great practical significance in terms of defense. Many castles were built in the Momoyama Period (1573–1600) when Japan was in the process of being unified militarily. If an invader managed to cross the moat, he had to pass through the main gate (Ōtemon) and follow a labyrinthine passage that included many gates and dead ends. There are three basic types of castle gates. The first, *kōraimon* (Korean style gate), has a gabled roof resting on posts. The second, *uzumimon* (embedded gate), is built directly into the walls of the castle, while the third, *yaguramon*, is a wooden structure with a hip-and-gable roof resting on a stone wall. *Uzumimon* gates, basically holes in the wall, could be sealed with dirt and gravel if the enemy attempted to force its way inside, and *yaguramon* gates could be

barred with heavy wooden doors reinforced with iron plates. The main gate played both a defensive and symbolic role in that its size and structure provided an indication of a *daimyo*'s influence and wealth.

In the Edo Period, commoners normally were forbidden to build residential gates. When average citizens began building gates for their private homes in the Meiji Period, they tended to be quite imposing to balance the large roofs of traditional houses. In recent years, there has been a tendency to construct residences with a more open and friendly design. A walled compound with an entrance gate, however, continues to be a popular status marker. Traditional style houses, as well as some modern homes, have small gardens, frequently set apart by an informal fence and entrance gate. The purpose of a residential garden and gate is not so much to impress others as to provide a sense of intimacy and relaxation in a busy world. Whereas formal entry gates are primarily for others, residential gardens and gates are for their owners.

Above: Beyond the *torii* (Shinto gate) is the Saidaimon (Large West Gate) of Usa Jingū in Kyushu (see pages 52–3). Remodeled around 1592 in the Momoyama Period, this colorful gate is in the *kirizuma* style (entrance on the long side rather than the gable end). The Chinese style pitched roof (*karahafu*) is covered with *hinoki* bark.

Left: The grand 20-*tatami* mat reception room at the Sukiya style Zanyūsō (literally, "a villa to enjoy oneself for a while") in Aichi Prefecture, built in 1917. The room offers a picture-perfect view of the garden and surrounding rooms.

Pre-Buddhist Cultures

In prehistoric times, people entered Japan from various parts of Asia. Originally hunters and gatherers, these early inhabitants eventually developed pottery, agriculture, permanent settlements, and increasingly sophisticated types of architecture. People were organized into clans, one of which gradually assumed dominance to establish the Yamato State and an imperial line that is still on the throne today.

1 Southern tip of Sakhalin
2 Shiraoi Ainu Village
 and Museum
3 Sannai Maruyama
 Jomon site
4 Fudodo Iseki
5 Ise Shrine
6 Kinki Area:
 • Yamato Region
 • Ikegami-sone
 • Nintoku's Tomb
7 Izumo Shrine
8 Yoshinogari Yayoi Site

Above: A flatland building (*heichi jūkyo*) in which poles were sloped to the top and thatched, serving as both walls and roof. The ground served as the floor.

Right: A flatland building reconstructed at the Ikegami-sone prehistoric site, Osaka Prefecture, in which the thatched roof is supported on walls made of reed-covered poles.

Pre-Ceramic Period (?–10000 BCE)

During the last Ice Age (Pleistocene Epoch), much of the water in the oceans was captured by glaciers, thereby lowering sea levels around the world. Some time before the end of the Pleistocene, when Kyushu and Hokkaido were still easily accessible from the Asian mainland because of low sea levels, different groups of hunting and gathering peoples entered Japan. Some entered southern Japan via the Korean Peninsula; some entered northern Japan via the northern island of Sakhalin; while others may have come directly from the south by boat.

Thus the Japanese people are not a homogeneous race as many believe. These early Paleolithic inhabitants had a variety of sophisticated stone tools but they lacked pottery or settled agriculture. Very little is known about their appearance or way of life, though archaeological evidence is gradually accumulating.

Jōmon Period (10000–300 BCE)

About 12,000 years ago, when the Ice Age ended, the climate warmed and sea levels climbed, cutting Japan off from the mainland. A new culture was born in the rapidly spreading deciduous forests, and pottery came into use. These ceramic people are called Jōmon (meaning "rope-marked") due to the practice of decorating their coil pottery by pressing a piece of rope into the damp surfaces of newly made vessels, some of which were utilitarian while others had wildly exuberant shapes. The Jōmon people continued the hunting and gathering way of life of their ancestors, supplemented by small-scale horticulture, including some grains. Recent evidence suggests that toward the end of the Jōmon Period, inhabitants in temperate regions of Japan may have experimented with wet rice agriculture on a small scale.

Jōmon buildings can be classified in different ways. According to one classification system, *heichi jūkyo* (flatland dwellings), originally developed in the pre-ceramic period, were simple structures in which the ground served as the floor; *tateana jūkyo* (pit dwellings) were roofs, or walls with roofs, constructed over circular or rectangular pits; and

hottatebashira tatemono (buildings with poles sunk in the ground) were larger buildings with a floor and a roof supported by a post-and-beam structure in which the posts were buried directly in the earth, rather than resting on rocks as in much of the architecture in later periods. Sometimes the floor of the latter was at ground level (*hiraya tatemono*), and at other times it was raised off the ground (*takayuka*), as in the case of storehouses or observation towers.

Pit houses were not suitable for wet areas or in places where there was inadequate drainage. Under the right conditions, however, pit houses helped provide protection against cold in the winter and heat in the summer.

Temporary flatland structures, pit houses, and raised floor structures all continued to be employed in the Yayoi Period and even persisted into historic times for use by commoners. Until recently, it was believed that elevated storehouses were first developed in the Yayoi Period. Recent findings, however, indicate that storehouses had earlier, Jōmon origins.

Yayoi Period (300 BCE–300 CE)

Around 300 BCE, or a little earlier, new people and cultural influences arrived from the Korean Peninsula, bringing metallurgy, large-scale wet rice agriculture based on irrigation, and wheel-made pottery. Originally centered in northern Kyushu, the Yayoi people initially appear to have fought the indigenous Jōmon people, but eventually mingled and interbred with them. This mixture provided the basis for the present-day Japanese people and culture.

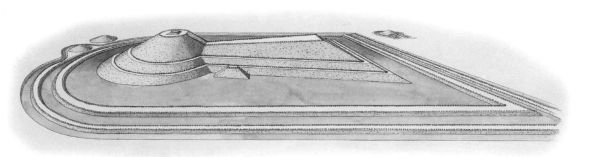

Left: Mound of Emperor Ninto-ku, the largest tomb mound in Japan. Surrounded by three moats, the mound has three terraces on which were placed rows of *haniwa* – ceramic figures in the shapes of humans, animals, buildings, etc. Drawing based on a model at the Osaka Prefectural Chikatsu Asuka Museum.

Many of the distinctive traits of Japanese culture date from these People of Wa, as they were called in early Chinese historical records. Some scholars believe that the Ainu, currently found only in Hokkaido and Sakhalin, may be descendants of a northern branch of the Jōmon people that escaped physical and cultural blending with the Yayoi people. The origins of the Ainu, however, are controversial.

The increased prosperity brought by the new way of life, with its intensive wet rice agriculture, created distinctions in wealth and an incipient class structure. An increase in population and social stratification eventually led to over 100 small states under the control of a variety of clans known as *uji*. The clan chief was both the secular and religious leader.

Tomb Mound Period (300–710 CE)

By 300 CE, one or more of the Yayoi *uji* appears to have gained some pre-eminence over the other clans, giving rise to a succession of imperial dynasties that culminated in the Yamato State of the mid-sixth century. The Yamato State, based in the area around the current cities of Nara, Kyoto, and Osaka (the Kinki area), controlled a large area, stretching from Kyushu in the west to the Kanto area in the east. The present imperial family of Japan, said to be the longest lived royal dynasty in the world, is believed to be descended from the ruling family of the Yamato State.

The Tomb Mound Period, which derives its name from the common practice of burying royalty and high-ranking clan officials in stone tombs covered with large earthen mounds, lasted from around 300 CE (or a little earlier) until 710. It thus overlaps with the coming of Buddhism in the middle of the sixth century. Buddhism, which was brought from China and Korea, introduced the advanced civilization of the continent, thereby bringing the prehistoric era to an end. Tomb mounds, however, continued to be built for another 200 years or so.

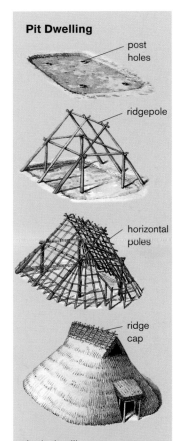

Pit Dwelling

post holes

ridgepole

horizontal poles

ridge cap

A pit dwelling was constructed by digging a hole about a meter deep and leaning poles against a rectangular framework to create sides. Thatch was tied to the reinforced sides, leaving openings at the top for smoke to escape.

Left: Elevated storehouses, used to protect rice, eventually developed into early Shinto shrines. Based on a model at the National Museum of Japanese History.

rat guard

Reconstructed Jōmon and Yayoi Settlements

Top and above: Exterior and interior of the large pit structure used for gatherings at the Fudōdō Iseki Jōmon site.

Below: Smoke hole in the roof of the Fudōdō Iseki pit structure.

Reconstructing the past is popular in Japan. The Japanese are intensely interested in their origins and are willing to travel to out-of-the way places to visit archaeological sites. Various levels of government have responded by investing heavily in reconstructing buildings and other architectural features at prehistoric sites, the most important of which are designated as National Historic Remains.

Sannai Maruyama Iseki

Sannai Maruyama Iseki in Aomori Prefecture (*iseki* means "remains") is the site of a Jōmon village that existed for around 1,500 years, from 3500 to 2000 BCE. Sannai Maruyama was situated on high ground overlooking Aomori Bay on the north. A road connected the center of the village and the eastern end of the high ground, with graves on both sides. In the center of the ceremonial space were a large pit dwelling, some smaller pit structures, and what may have been a large lookout tower, described below. So far, archaeologists have uncovered the remains of 800 pit dwellings, 120 post-and-beam structures (such as elevated storage buildings and observation towers), and over 10,000 holes, whose use is uncertain.

Though intact timbers no longer remain, a good deal can be inferred from excavated post holes. For example, excavated post holes indicate the circumference and height of the trees used. In one excavation, the bottoms of the holes slope in such a way that the poles must have leaned toward each other. Poles sloping in this way would have been unstable unless connected by a raised platform, and possibly a roof. It is inferred that this structure may have been used as a lookout tower. Remains of wood found in the holes are from large chestnut trees, probably raised for the nuts.

The findings at Sannai Maruyama have forced scholars to change their ideas about Jōmon communities. Contrary to earlier beliefs that Jōmon people had a primitive lifestyle based upon hunting wild animals, the residents of Sannai Maruyama settled in one place for an extended period of time, cultivated some food such as chestnuts, imported goods by boat from different parts of Japan, buried their dead, and lived at peace with their neighbors. So far, reconstruction has been completed on one large and five small pit dwellings, three raised floor structures, and one large structure consisting of posts sunk in the ground (perhaps used as a lookout), which may have had a roof. A committee of experts from the fields

of architecture, archaeology, and ethnology are continuing research on how to proceed with reconstruction.

Fudōdō Iseki

Situated at the northeastern corner of Toyama Prefecture, the Fudōdō site dates from around 3000 BCE. Excavations started in 1973 and so far have uncovered 19 house sites, nine deep holes which seem to have been used for storing food, and numerous earthen and stoneware vessels. Especially notable is the evidence of a huge oval-shaped pit building, measuring 8 by 17 meters, in the middle of the settlement. Because this is four to five times larger than an average house site, and has four sets of stone structures for cooking, it is believed that this building was used for gatherings. This meeting hall and two other buildings have been reconstructed so far.

Yoshinogari Iseki

Yoshinogari, in Saga Prefecture, Kyushu, is situated on a low hill bordered by a river on two sides. Excavations, begun in 1986, have uncovered habitation sites spanning the entire Yayoi Period (300 BCE–300 CE). By the latter part of the mid-Yayoi Period, a large-scale settlement guarded by surrounding moats was in place. Excavations have uncovered numerous skeletons buried in ceramic urns and a rich material culture, including bronze implements and glass beads. Both skeletons and material remains indicate a Korean origin.

By the late Yayoi Period, Yoshinogari possessed two smaller areas within the larger area, marked off by inner moats and fences. The most important buildings were located in these smaller areas, one on the south and one on the north. In 1986, two watchtowers and three pit houses were reconstructed in the south fenced area, as well as two raised storage buildings to the west of this fenced area.

Reconstruction of the north fenced area has been under way since 1999. This area, which contains several buildings, was probably the compound of a chief. It includes a pit house and several raised structures, one of which is a large building believed to be an early shrine. The other raised buildings include what appear to be lookout towers, storehouses, and a structure that the chief may have used for residential, political, religious, and ceremonial functions – an early form of a palace. It would have been difficult, however, to construct a fire pit in a raised structure, so cooking was probably confined to the pit house. In later times, new methods of containing fire allowed cooking to be done in raised buildings.

In recognition of the fact that it was the largest Yayoi settlement surrounded by moats and that it probably developed into a key component of the emerging Yamato State, Yoshinogari has been designated as a Special National Historic Remain.

Ikegami-sone Iseki

This Yayoi site, in Osaka Prefecture, is located on a low hill surrounded by a moat, with rivers (that no longer exist) to the east and west. As at Yoshinogari, there is a smaller enclosed area that seems to have been set aside for the chief, as well as factory areas for making stone tools and other products.

A large-scale excavation was done in 1969–71, leading to the designation, in 1976, of Ikegami-sone Iseki as a National Historic Remain. In 1994, archaeologists discovered the remains of a large building with a floor area of 130 square meters. A distinguishing feature of this building is the use of thick posts to support the roof at both ends, in the fashion of a shrine. Parts of the 17 posts used in the building are still in the ground. Using modern dating methods, it has been determined that one of the posts was cut in 52 BCE. So far, one pit house and two elevated post-and-beam buildings have been reconstructed.

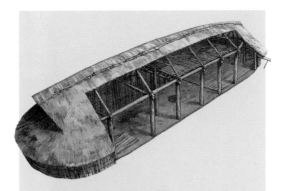

Long House at Sannai Maruyama

Archaeologists have uncovered the remains of 800 pit structures and 120 post-and-beam structures at Sannai Maruyama. The long house shown here, based on a model at the National Museum of Japanese History, is the largest of the pit structures. Because of its size, it is believed to be a public building used for meetings and ceremonies. The massive roof rests on walls, unlike most small pit structures in which the roof rests directly on the ground.

Changing Conceptions

It was long thought that the Jōmon people lived a simple hunting and gathering lifestyle that required only simple buildings and tools. In contrast, it was believed that the Yayoi people brought a much more sophisticated

Below: Yoshinogari is a very large Yayoi site containing two smaller areas for the most important structures, one on the north and one on the south. Depicted here are the buildings that were reconstructed in the south area in 1986. They are enclosed by a fence on top of a high earthen wall and two moats. There are entrances at both ends and watchtowers on both sides. Elevated storehouses and numerous pit dwellings lie outside the enclosed area.

culture with them from the mainland, including agriculture and more advanced forms of tools, weapons, and architecture. As a result, it was long assumed that Yayoi culture rapidly displaced the more primitive Jōmon culture.

Though there is undoubtedly some truth in this generalization, the distinction between Jōmon and Yayoi cultures should not be over-emphasized. Recent findings indicate that although Yayoi villages were more heavily fortified and exhibit a greater degree of social stratification, Jōmon villages were sometimes quite large, diverse, and persisted over considerable periods of time. Moreover, Jōmon people traveled long distances by boat, engaging in trade with areas as far apart

Above: Ceremonial building at the Ikegami-sone reconstructed Yayoi site. The members of the structure are tied together (see right), as was common in prehistoric buildings and later farmhouses. Since rope can stretch, such buildings could move during a typhoon without causing serious damage. Next to the building is a covered well, made from a hollowed-out camphor tree, probably used for purification ceremonies connected with the large building. Photograph above courtesy of Izumi City.

Right: Reconstructed shrine from the northern enclosure at Yoshinogari. Like the elevated storehouses, the shrine was constructed on posts sunk in the ground. It also may have had some of the features of later Shinto shrines, such as verandas that encircled the interior space. The actual appearance of the building, however, is conjectural. For example, it is impossible to know whether it had two stories, as indicated in the reconstruction, or a single story, as in the case of later shrines, such as those at Ise.

as Hokkaido and western Honshu. Imported items included jade and obsidian implements, fish, and asphalt. The latter was mixed with clay to make utensils, and to decorate clay figurines. The Jōmon people also cultivated chestnuts and appear to have experimented with growing other crops such as a dry land form of rice.

One of the most interesting findings is that there also is considerable continuity between Jōmon and Yayoi architecture. For example, it was long assumed that elevated storehouses began in the Yayoi Period. It is now known that elevated Yayoi storehouses, which later developed into shrines and palaces, were a continuation of an earlier Jōmon tradition.

Evidence Used in Reconstructions

Reconstructing what buildings may have looked like at Yoshinogari and other prehistoric sites involves educated guesswork based upon archaeological evidence, designs on bronze mirrors and bells, designs on earthenware pots, and clay models (*haniwa*) of buildings that have been found in concentric rings on the slopes of tomb mounds. Clues can also be obtained from contemporary ethnographic evidence such as Shinto shrines that have periodically been rebuilt over the centuries, the construction methods used in centuries-old farmhouses, temporary structures that were used until recently for a variety of purposes such as birthing, and architectural styles still found in other parts of Asia that supplied immigrants to Japan in prehistoric times. Piecing these various kinds of data together requires a high degree of teamwork.

Top: Archaeologists working at the Yoshinogari Yayoi site in Kyushu.

Above: *Iegata haniwa* (house-shaped clay model) found at the Saitobaru site in Miyazaki Prefecture.

Above: Pot in the Osaka Prefectural Museum of Yayoi Culture, from the Karako site in Nara Prefecture, depicting a raised structure.

The Grand Shrines at Ise

The architectural significance of the Ise shrines is that they are an early example of some of the basic principles of architecture now considered to be typically Japanese, such as using thatch for roofing and exposed, unpainted wood for beams and walls, raising the structure on wooden posts, and adapting a building to the natural environment. Of the ancient shrines in Japan, Ise Jingū is the most important.

Shinto

The clan chief in prehistoric times was also the clan head of a religion that eventually came to be known as Shinto, the Way of the Gods. Shinto is based upon the belief that there is a divine power in nature (*kami*) that permeates everything but is more highly concentrated in some things, such as particular waterfalls, trees, animals, people, ancestral spirits, and even human artifacts. Often, Shinto shrines are located near natural phenomena, such as a sacred mountain, where there is an especially high concentration of divine power. The term *kami* also is used in reference to mythological deities such as Amaterasu-Ōmikami, the sun goddess, from whom the imperial line is said to be descended.

Despite the abstract nature of *kami*, specific concentrations of power assume the characteristics of individual deities that can be offered domicile in shrine buildings dedicated to them. Thus, when individuals visit shrines, they pay respects to particular *kami* rather than to an abstract divine power.

Shinto ceremonies are organized around the concept of purification. Blood, death, and disease are highly polluting and must be cleansed if an individual is to communicate with the divine. Ceremonies can be as simple as washing one's hands and mouth at a water basin before praying at a shrine, or as complicated as participating in a full-scale ceremony conducted by a priest, replete with traditional music and dancing by shrine maidens.

Pre-Buddhist Shrines

The three main types of shrine architecture from the Pre-Buddhist period are the Taisha, Sumiyoshi, and Shimmei styles. The Taisha style is represented by Izumo Shrine in Shimane Prefecture. In prehistoric times, Izumo Shrine was situated on a high platform reached by a long flight of steps. According to records kept at the shrine, the original building was 96 meters high, which was later reduced to 48 meters, and eventually to 24 meters, because of the building's tendency to collapse without any apparent cause. Kan-ari Matsuri, a festival

Right: The main compound (viewed from the south) of the Naikū at Ise Jingū consists of a sanctuary and two treasure houses enclosed by a series of fences. Omitted in the drawing is a small covered annex that protects participants in ceremonies conducted outside the entrance to the sanctuary. To the west of the compound is another white graveled lot where the new Naikū will be located when the present structures are dismantled.

treasure houses

main shrine

entrance

for all the Shinto gods in Japan, is celebrated annually at Izumo from October 11 through 17. Since there are no gods at the other shrines during this period, October is known as *kannazuki* (godless month) in the rest of Japan.

The Sumiyoshi style, represented by Sumiyoshi Shrine in the city of Osaka, consists of four gable-entrance structures overlooking the sea. The Grand Shrines at Ise, on the Kii Peninsula, Mie Prefecture, represent the Shimmei style.

The Setting at Ise

There are two shrine compounds at Ise, located several kilometers apart: the inner or Naikū dedicated to the sun goddess, and the outer or Gekū dedicated to the goddess of food, Toyo-uke-Ōmikami.

Despite some minor differences, the styles of the Naikū and Gekū are almost identical. Collectively known as Ise Jingū, the shrines are situated in an ancient cedar forest. Although the main buildings of both the inner and outer shrines are separated from the world by a series of fences that bar most people from entering, the main features of the architecture can be seen in the numerous subsidiary buildings found throughout the two compounds. Basically, the buildings are derived from raised prehistoric rice storehouses that were gradually modified and refined into some of the world's most highly sophisticated structures.

Above: Pre-Buddhist Izumo Taisha, 48 meters high, based on a model at Koyama Industrial High School, which relies on a painting kept at Izumo Shrine and on research by architectural historian Fukuyama Toshio.

Above left: Detail of a picture scroll by Ikebe Gishō depicting a visit to Ise Jingū by the Emperor Taishō on November 14, 1916, four years after he ascended the throne. The procession is passing through the *torii* (Shinto arches) and thatched gateways to the main shrine compound.

Left: In the background is one of the shrine buildings at Ise Jingū. In the foreground is the graveled area where an exact copy will be reconstructed when the complex is replaced.

Right: Kagura-den complex at the Naikū, Ise Jingū, where sacred dances and music are performed. Unlike the shrines on the grounds, which are built in the *kirizuma* style (thatched gable roofs), the Kagura-den has a hipped-and-gable roof (*irimoya* style) with copper shingles. See page 39 for roof styles.

Right: Interior of a shrine at Takachiho in Kyushu where Ninigi-no-Mikoto, grandson of the sun goddess, is said to have descended to a nearby mountain. On the altar is a mirror representing one of the three symbols of divine authority (the other two being the sword and the jewel) received from the sun goddess herself.

The "Historical" Record

According to tradition, long ago, in the Age of the Gods, Ninigi-no-Mikoto, grandson of the sun goddess Amaterasu-Ōmikami, was presented with a mirror by his grandmother and sent to rule over the land of Japan. His grandmother informed him that the mirror would serve as a symbol of her presence. Ninigi took a beautiful goddess as his consort, but when he refused to take an older, ugly sister as well, the father put a curse on Ninigi's offspring so their lives would be short. Thus the human race was born. Succeeding emperors kept Ninigi's sacred mirror in their palaces, where it was worshipped as a manifestation of the sun goddess. Some time in the latter part of the third century CE, during the final years of the Yayoi Period, the eleventh emperor, Suinin, built a permanent shrine for the mirror and ordered the princess Toyo-sukiiri-hime-no-mikoto to serve the sun goddess as the representative of the imperial family. This system of having a "princess-shaman" as head priest at Ise remained in effect until the Muromachi Period (1333–1573).

Rebuilding Program

The shrines are rebuilt every 20 years, a policy begun by the Emperor Temmu in 685, over a century after the formal introduction of Buddhism and the invasion of Chinese culture. It was probably to guard against such growing influence that the rebuilding program was instituted. While many other shrines were rapidly adopting Chinese characteristics, such as curved roofs and painted wood, the straight-line Shimmei style and the use of natural materials was maintained at Ise. Some features, however, such as the metal fittings, the north–south orientation of the buildings, and the design of the gates, appear to be due to continental influence.

The rebuilding program requires a massive expenditure of resources, time, and money since it involves replacing 65 structures and approximately 16,000 artifacts that fill them. This requires a small army of carpenters, thatchers, sculptors, metal workers, cloth makers, and other craftspeople. The rebuilding program commences 12 years after the completion of the preceding program and takes 8 years to complete. It is accompanied by 32 major rituals – beginning with cutting nearly 14,000 *hinoki* (Japanese cypress or white cedar) trees

Below: This wooden lantern on the grounds of Ise Jingū harmonizes with the architectural style of the complex.

Main Sanctuary at the Naikū

The main sanctuary at the Naikū is a raised rectangular structure, three bays wide by two bays deep, made of *hinoki* (Japanese cypress) harvested from a forest preserve deep in the mountains. The unpainted wood gradually changes in color over its 20-year life span, from golden brown to gray. Perhaps the most impressive feature is the large roof thatched with the stems of a mountain reed. The roof ridge is supported by two free-standing pillars sunk directly into the earth in the *hottatebashira* style used in preceding Jōmon and Yayoi elevated storehouses. The walls also rest upon heavy pillars that support the raised floor, which is surrounded by a graceful veranda with a handrail. A sacred post stands under the middle of the floor, above which the sacred mirror is kept in a container resting on a stand. The entrance is in the middle of one of the long sides, a style called *hirairi*. To avoid an imbalance, the roof thatch narrows as it rises, as do the huge pillars that support the ridgepole. At each end of the roof, the roof poles cross and extend beyond to form the *chigi* (forked finials). This helps balance the massive outward slope of the roof. Laid across the ridgepole is a row of long, close-set pegs, the *katsuogi* – ten at the Naikū and nine at the Gekū, reflecting their difference in status. The long slender pegs extending from the gable ends, four on each side of the ridgepole, are known as *muchikake*.

from an imperial forest preserve in the Kiso mountains of Nagano Prefecture. The trees are floated down the river to a site on the Ise Jingū grounds where priest-carpenters employ ancient tools and rituals to begin fashioning timbers for the new buildings. Thatching the new shrines requires around 25,000 bundles of mountain reeds (*kaya*).

Major buildings are built on adjoining lots where structures from the previous 20-year cycle were dismantled. At the center of each vacant lot is a miniature wooden building that covers a *hinoki* stick that marks the spot where the sacred "heart pillar" under the center of the new building will be erected. The newly constructed buildings are supposed to be exact copies of the old shrines. After the new shrines have been authenticated by the priests, the old shrines are torn down and

their materials are given to tributary shrines throughout Japan. This method ensures a faithful transmission of the old style. Although there have been several lapses in this rebuilding program, the shrines at Ise Jingū were rebuilt for the 61st time in 1993.

Above: Painting of a pilgrimage to Ise. Pilgrimages became very popular during the Edo Period since travel was safe and people had more money than in previous periods. In 1830, for example, 4,600,000 people visited Ise during a six-month period. Sometimes, those who could not make the pilgrimage sent their dogs with friends or relatives to be blessed by the priests at Ise. This illustration is a detail from a scroll by Tanaka Ekishin, housed in the Jingū Chōkokan Museum near Ise Jingū. Photograph courtesy of the Jingū Chōkokan Museum.

Ainu Buildings

Above: Early photograph by Kinoshita Seizō, showing an Ainu couple in traditional costume in front of their house.

Until recently, the Ainu, the indigenous people of northern Japan, lived in small, seasonal settlements (*kotan*), located in food-gathering areas. For example, in spring they lived along the seashore where they collected fish and seaweed; in summer they lived in the mountains where they hunted animals and collected wild vegetables and berries; and in winter they lived in valleys protected from wind and snow.

Traditional Dwellings

The simplest type of dwelling was a *kashi*. It consisted of a tripod whose sides were covered with branches and woven mats. It was large enough to provide shelter from the rain for a family of four or five. When more room was needed, a beam was placed between two sets of tripods and the sides enclosed to create a *kucha*, which housed up to 10 people.

A *chise*, a larger house with a roof set on walls, allowed enough space to stand up, make a fire, and do other kinds of indoor work. Upon entering a *chise* from the *semu* (entrance and storage area), one found a large room with small windows and an earth floor, in the middle of which was a square fire pit with mats on both sides. On one side of the room was a raised area on which were placed articles such as lacquer boxes and sacred objects made of shaved wood (*inaw*). Hanging from the smoke-blackened rafters were bows and arrows for hunting.

Traditionally, *chise* were constructed on a river bank so the sacred objects could face upstream where the gods were believed to reside. A *chise* lasted around 10 years or longer, depending upon how well it was constructed and maintained.

The *chise* house shown in the drawing on this page has walls and roof consisting of bundles of reeds or bamboo grass attached to poles tied horizontally to the main frame. Smoke holes are left at the top. The ridge is covered with a cap weighted down with wooden poles that are tied to the rafters. To the left of the main building are two toilets, one for males and one for females. To the right of the building is a cage where a bear cub was raised until it was large enough to be killed in the most important of the Ainu ceremonies. The slain bear was eaten in a ritual feast and its skull adorned and honored. To the right of the bear cage is a small, elevated storehouse, reminiscent of Jōmon *kura*. In the foreground is a garden, behind which is a drying rack. Vegetables were supplemented by salmon and wild meat such as deer.

Winter houses, called *toi-chise*, "house of dirt," were built by erecting a roof over a pit and covering it with earth to retain the heat. This type of house was observed in Sakhalin as late as 1946. Dwellings in spring and summer villages were built with less substantial materials, such as poles covered with reeds or grass.

Right: A traditional Ainu house with entrance/storage room attached to a larger room. The house shown here is based on a model at the National Museum of Ethnology, Osaka.

Construction of a Poro-chise Building

When the *poro-chise* (large house) at the Ainu
Museum in Shiraoi, Hokkaido, burned in 1996,
the museum staff undertook its reconstruction
using traditional building principles they had
learned from elders over the years. First, vertical
posts were buried in the ground, and purlins
were attached to the top to create the walls.
Ceiling beams were used to connect the two
side walls to create a solid framework. For the
roof, two tripods were erected on top of the
frame and connected with a ridgepole, leaving
smoke holes at both ends. Rafters were run
from the wall purlins to the ridgepole, and small
poles were attached horizontally across the
rafters. The finished roof was covered with fish-
nets, and overlapping reed bundles were tied
vertically to the roof frame, starting with the bottom row. Reed bundles on the top row were
bent over the ridge and covered with additional
small bundles to create a unique ridge shape.
Small horizontal poles were fastened on the
outside of the vertical wall posts for attaching
reed bundles to build the walls. More small
poles were attached horizontally over the reeds
to help hold them in place. Window holes were
cut and fitted with coverings that are pulled
by ropes from inside to close the openings.

Poro-chise (large house) building under
construction at Shiraoi in 1996. The floor
and walls of the finished house have
been covered with mats. The roof beams
remain exposed. The shelf on the wall
is for holding ceremonial objects. A
large spark deflector hangs over the
recessed fire pit.

Traditional Religion

Traditional Ainu religion was organized around
a cult in which a bear cub was captured and
raised by an Ainu woman. In recent times, the
cub was raised in a cage until grown, when it
was ritually killed and eaten in the Iyomante
ceremony. The skull was adorned, worshipped,
and paraded through the village in a rite designed to free the spirit of the bear and to
maintain good relations with the spirit world.

Decline of Traditional Culture

The traditional way of life of the Ainu continued until around the end of the Edo Period.
In 1899, the government enacted the Hokkaido Ainu Preservation Law, encouraging the
Ainu to live in permanent villages and to culti-
vate the land. However, there was little land
available, as Japanese (Wa-jin) had been immi-
grating to Hokkaido since the fifteenth century. Laws prohibiting traditional customs and
food-gathering practices led to the decline of
traditional culture and language, as well as
to an overall lower standard of living.

In the twentieth century, the Hokkaido
prefectural government established housing
programs for the Ainu, but the houses were
so small and poorly built that the Ainu preferred to live in traditional style houses next
to the government buildings. In 1997, the
Diet passed a new law advocating research
on Ainu culture and supporting the preservation of Ainu language, customs, and traditions.
It remains to be seen if this law will improve
the situation of the Ainu. Ainu leaders are
attempting to revitalize traditional culture by
teaching the Ainu language and traditional
customs to young people. There are only a
few elders, however, who possess this kind
of knowledge, so the task is daunting and
the outcome is uncertain.

There are around 24 reconstructed *chise*
in Hokkaido, and three more in other areas.
However, none are actually used as living
quarters at present. The way of life of contemporary Ainu is not that much different from
that of the larger population, into which they
have, for the most part, been assimilated.

Influences from Korea and China

Buddhism was introduced to Japan in the sixth century from the Korean state of Paekche. The sophisticated new religion was welcomed by the Yamato Court as a way to help promote a stronger centralized government. A great flowering of architecture ensued as magnificent temples, filled with statues and other works of art, were built to impress people at home and abroad.

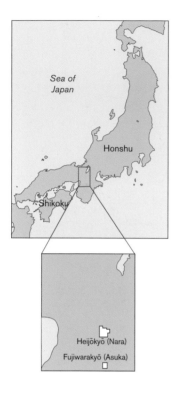

Below: This storehouse at Tōdaiji, from the Nara Period, consists of triangular logs that expand in the summer to keep moisture out and contract in the winter to allow air circulation.

Asuka Period (538–645)

The traditional date for the introduction of Buddhism to Japan is 538, although the date 552 is often used as well. The period between the arrival of Buddhism and the Taika Reform of 645 is known as the Asuka Period. The Asuka Period takes its name from the Asuka area near Nara, the site of the first real capital. During the Asuka Period, Japan was thoroughly transformed as it came under the influence of continental civilization.

When Buddhism was introduced, controversy erupted between the Mononobe and Soga clans concerning whether the new religion should be adopted officially or whether Shinto should retain a dominant position. This debate came at a time when Japan was evolving rapidly from a federation of influential clans into a nation under a centralized government known as the Yamato State. The Soga clan, which favored the official adoption of Buddhism, prevailed and the Yamato Court decided to use Buddhism as a political tool to help consolidate its power.

Prince Shōtoku, who was appointed Regent by the Empress Suiko in 593, was more interested in the religious and philosophical aspects of Buddhism than in its use as a political tool. He became a devout follower and actively promoted the new religion. Under his patronage, great numbers of Korean craftspeople came to Japan to build Buddhist temples and furnish them with sculpture, paintings, and the decorative arts. The two main compounds constructed by Prince Shōtoku were Hōryūji Temple near Nara and Shitennōji Temple in Osaka.

The first temple, however, was Hōkōji, later called Asukadera (*tera*, or *dera*, means "temple") by local residents because of its location. It was constructed in 596 by Sogano-Umako, with the help of the Korean king of Paekche. Most of the buildings were moved to Nara in 718 and renamed Gangōji, but the central object of worship, a statue of the historical Buddha (Shaka), was left behind, where it still exists in a newer building. Though badly damaged and in poor repair, the image is of great historical interest since it was the first Buddhist statue in Japan.

Hakuhō Period (645–710)

The Taika Reform of 645 created a central government with a legislative structure based upon the model of Tang China. Official interchange with China was established for the first time and envoys were exchanged between the two courts. Buddhist architecture, arts, and crafts spread from the capital to the provinces, and literature flourished, as evidenced by the publication of a great collection of 4,400 poems, the *Manyōshū*.

In the early days, the capital was moved every time an emperor died. In 694, the Emperor Temmu decided to build a permanent capital at Fujiwarakyō (*kyō* means capital city), a little north of Asuka. The capital for seven years, it was the first full-scale capital in Japan, with streets laid out in a square grid pattern, as was the custom in China. However, changes in the political and economic situation made it necessary to expand the government bureaucracy. Because the space at Fujiwarakyō was limited, the capital was moved to Heijōkyō (the present-day Nara) in 710 by the Emperor Genmei.

Nara Period (710–794)

Despite several temporary moves back and forth between Heijōkyō and other locations, Heijōkyō remained the capital for 74 years With official support, the major Buddhist denominations built headquarters in Heijōkyō, such as Yakushiji and Kōfukuji. Emperor Shōmu, a vigorous supporter of Buddhism, decreed that temples and nunneries be erected in each province and that Tōdaiji be built in

smoke hole

raised floor

earthen floor

Heijōkyō as the head cathedral of this national network. Tōdaiji housed a great bronze Buddha (Daibutsu) that still exists today. In 752, dignitaries from as far away as Persia gathered for the eye-opening ceremony, during which the eyes were painted in by an eminent Indian priest.

A number of items used by Emperor Shōmu in his daily life are preserved in the Shōsōin Repository of Imperial Treasures in Nara, one of the few buildings still remaining from the Nara Period. The great flowering of architecture and the arts in the Nara Period marks the high point of Buddhist culture in Japan.

Recycling
In 718, Asukadera Temple (in Asuka), the first temple in Japan, was dismantled and the lumber was used to build Gangōji Temple in Heijōkyō. Gangōji burned in 1451 but some of the original lumber from Asukadera

Temple was salvaged and used in reconstructing the Meditation Hall (Zenshitsu), which still exists today. Thus, the Meditation Hall of Gangōji contains lumber that predates Hōryūji, the oldest extant wooden structure in the world.

Residential Architecture
The sixth through the eighth centuries are best known for the introduction of Buddhism and the construction of capitals in the Chinese style, as described above. There were, how-ever, indigenous developments, primarily in the area of residential architecture. Average houses were probably post-and-beam structures, with either thatch or board roofs, the latter weighted down with stones. Starting in the Asuka Period, palaces, temples, and aristocratic dwellings were built at the expense of the farmers who paid heavy taxes and provided forced labor. Farmhouses grew progressively smaller as the condition of farmers worsened.

At the same time, however, technology improved to the point that it was possible to eliminate interior posts that supported the roofs of pit houses and rely solely on pillars in the exterior walls. Eventually, the pit was eliminated altogether in favor of rectangular ground-level dwellings with two interior rooms: a room with an earthen floor and fire pit for cooking, and a room whose earthen floor was covered with straw and mats for eating and sleeping. This basic plan can still be seen in some traditional farmhouses, known as *minka*.

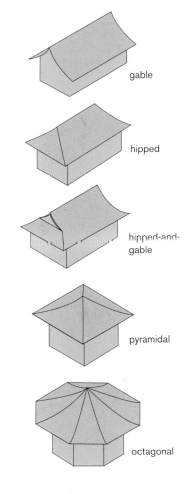

gable

hipped

hipped-and-gable

pyramidal

octagonal

Left: Only the foundations remain from the original buildings at Shitennōji, one of the earliest temples in Japan. This model at the Osaka Prefectural Chikatsu Asuka Museum shows the linear arrangement of the gate, pagoda, main hall, and lecture hall.

Right: Tōdaiji Temple, one of the seven great temples of Nara, was established as a center for Buddhism, newly introduced from China, in the eighth century. Its architecture was influenced by the grand scale of Buddhist architecture of China's Tang Dynasty, especially in the size of its Daibutsuden (Great Hall) and the large, heavy roof and complex bracketing system that supported it. The present Daibutsuden, although still grand, is significantly smaller than the original, which was twice destroyed by fire. Still the largest wooden building in the world under one roof, it houses the Great Buddha.

Heijōkyō: An Early Capital

Above: Model of an ornamental roof tile used on a corner of the roof of the second Daigokuden. The tile is called *onigawara* (tile with a "devil" face). The face shown here is a good devil, whose job was to frighten away bad devils that caused fire, lightning, wind, and other damage to buildings.

Early capitals were temporary affairs that were moved when an emperor died. Needing to demonstrate the power of the Yamato Court, Emperor Genmei decided to move the capital from Fujiwarakyō, near Asuka, to Heijōkyō, a site considered ideal according to Chinese principles of geomancy. The move, accomplished in only two years, was facilitated by dismantling the existing palace and reusing the lumber.

The City

In 708, when the emperor decided to move the capital to Heijōkyō (*kyō* means capital), the people living in the area had to be relocated. Hills had to be leveled and valleys filled in, with much of the work done by conscripted farmers working with hand tools. The work was so difficult that many attempted to escape and return home. Heijōkyō, modeled after the Chinese capital of Ch'angan, occupied an area 5.9 kilometers from east to west and 4.8 kilometers from north to south; 1.2 square kilometers were allotted for the palace. For materials, they moved lumber and tile from the Fujiwara palace, supplemented by timbers brought from neighboring prefectures on rafts floated down the river to the nearby town of Kizu. Stone was quarried at Nijōzan, a mountain near the present Nara City, and tile was manufactured at kilns near the new capital.

Heijōkyō was a good-sized city with an estimated population of around 100,000. The city was divided into squares, with streets running north and south and avenues running east and west. Heijōkyū, the palace compound, was placed at the northern end of the capital, as in Ch'angan, the capital of Tang China, and was enclosed by a 5-meter-high fence. The main street of the capital was a 74-meter-wide thoroughfare, Suzaku Ōji, which ran from Suzakumon, the main palace gate, to Rajōmon, a gate at the southern entrance of the capital. Outside the palace compound were temples, houses, and the east and west market areas. Commerce was allowed only in the market areas, controlled by the government, which brought goods in via canals and the Akishino River, which passed by the west market.

Except for several short-lived moves to other cities, Heijōkyō remained the capital of Japan for 74 years until the capital was moved to Nagaokakyō in 784 and then to Heiankyō (Kyoto) in 794 where it remained for around 1,000 years.

The Palace

The main buildings in the palace area were the Daigokuden (Hall of State), in which national events such as coronation ceremonies and meetings with foreign delegations took place, and the Chōdōin (government offices). These buildings were Chinese in style, constructed on raised platforms, some of which

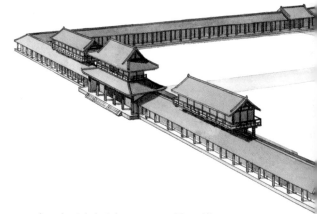

were faced with brick or stone. Vermilion colored posts supporting the large tiled roof rested on foundation stones. Some of the bays between these posts were open, while others were closed in with white plastered walls.

To the north of the Daigokuden, inside a fenced area, was the Dairi, the emperor's living quarters. Although there is little detailed information about palaces and aristocratic mansions from this period, they seem to have been constructed in the indigenous Japanese style, consisting of a large, undivided central area (*moya*), part of which was enclosed by walls or doors, with the rest open to one or more raised verandas that were sometimes covered with their own roofs to form extensions

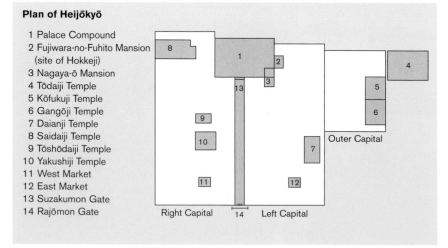

Plan of Heijōkyō

1 Palace Compound
2 Fujiwara-no-Fuhito Mansion (site of Hokkeji)
3 Nagaya-ō Mansion
4 Tōdaiji Temple
5 Kōfukuji Temple
6 Gangōji Temple
7 Daianji Temple
8 Saidaiji Temple
9 Tōshōdaiji Temple
10 Yakushiji Temple
11 West Market
12 East Market
13 Suzakumon Gate
14 Rajōmon Gate

Outer Capital

Right Capital   Left Capital

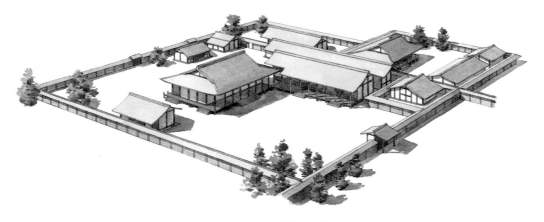

Left: Detail from a model at the Nara Bunkazai Kenkyūjo (Nara National Cultural Properties Research Institute) of the mansion of Nagayaō, Minister of the Left at the beginning of the Nara Period. The Nagayaō mansion was an early form of the Shinden style that became popular in the following Heian Period. It had an elevated plank floor surrounded by a raised veranda, and post-and-beam construction (with the main posts buried in the ground) that made it possible to use sliding doors. Most buildings had shingled or bark-covered roofs but some may have been tiled.

known as *hisashi*. The floor was raised and planked, and the bark roof was either hipped or hipped-and-gable. The main posts were sunk in the ground in the *hottatebashira* fashion used since prehistoric times, rather than resting on foundation stones. In the Nara Period, these aristocratic residences developed into Shinden style mansions, which take their

Class Structure

Government workers were organized into eight ranks. Those in the first five ranks, numbering only about 150, were considered aristocrats, a status conferred by birth. There were about 10,000 bureaucrats in the bottom three ranks and another 10,000 without rank. There was a large gap between the 5th and 6th ranks

Left: The first Daigokudenin (Courtyard of the Hall of State) at Heijōkyō, based on a model at the Nara Bunkazai Kenkyūjo. The first Daigokuden was dismantled and relocated when the capital was moved temporarily in 740. When the capital was moved back to Heijōkyō in 745, a second Daigokuden was built to the east of the first one.

name from the main hall (*shinden*). The *shinden*, the residence of the household head, was flanked on both sides by subsidiary buildings.

Fujiwara-no-Fuhito, Minister of the Right and the real power behind the imperial court, was the one who oversaw the move of the capital from Fujiwarakyō to Heijōkyō. He was anxious to set the stage for his grandson, Obito-no-Ōji (later the Emperor Shōmu), to ascend the throne and expand the Fujiwara power base. Obito-no-Ōji's palace was constructed in the eastern part of the palace grounds, and the vast residence of Fujiwara-no-Fuhito was built next to this area on the east, but outside the walls.

since bureaucrats could not become aristocrats. Moreover, aristocrats led lives of relative luxury whereas bureaucrats practically lived at their places of work.

Land was allotted according to rank, ranging from four *cho* of land (one *cho* was 2.451 acres) for the upper ranks to 250 square meters for unranked bureaucrats. Low-ranking bureaucrats and ordinary people lived in urban dwellings similar to rural farmhouses (*minka*), consisting of a pit house and one or two buildings that may have been used as workshops or storehouses. It was not until the following Heian Period that town houses, known as *machiya*, were specially developed for merchants and artisans.

Hōryūji: The Oldest Extant Temple

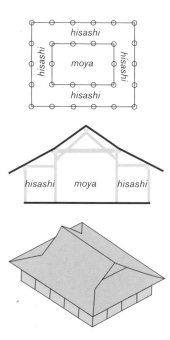

Above: Buddhist structures employ a post-and-lintel technique in which the eaves of the roof are cantilevered over the verandas by brackets that rest on lintels. The interior of the building (*moya*) consists of an odd number of bays in width by two in depth. Surrounding the *moya* are areas one bay in width which are known as *hisashi*.

Hōryūji in Nara is the most important temple in Japan, due to its great antiquity, beauty, and architectural integrity. Other extant remains from the temples of early Japan consist of single buildings, or parts of buildings. At Hōryūji, nearly the entire complex has been preserved, providing a priceless insight into the basic principles of continental Buddhist architecture in the early historic period.

Buddhist Architectural Innovations

Buddhism, with its sophisticated doctrines and universal appeal, was a radical departure from the relatively simple nature worship of Shinto; its architecture was radically different as well. First, Chinese Buddhist architecture was based upon cosmological principles that required a strict, usually symmetrical, layout of the temple compound, surrounded by a wall and entered through a formal gateway. In contrast, early Shinto shrines attempted to fit into nature. Secondly, early Buddhist temples were complex and highly ornamental. Buildings were often constructed on a raised earthen podium. Foundation stones, partially buried in the stone-faced, packed earth floors, provided a base for large pillars that held up a massive tiled roof with a complex system of brackets to support the extensive overhang. Posts were colored vermilion, and the spaces between the posts were filled with white plastered walls. The interior was lavishly decorated and often included a magnificent altar.

In contrast, early Shinto shrines were quite simple in basic design. The roof, while large, was covered with thatch or bark and thus was not heavy enough to require a complex support system. Posts were often planted directly in the earth and the wood was left in its natural state. Interiors were equally austere.

Over time, imported and indigenous styles of religious architecture influenced each other, with the result that many Shinto shrines assumed more elaborate forms and brighter colors, while many Buddhist temples evolved in the direction of greater simplicity and made a conscious attempt to fit into the natural surroundings.

Four Basic Types of Temples

The original building techniques brought from Korea and China were altered to suit a different environment in Japan, such as strengthening joints to make the building more resistant to earthquakes and typhoons. These early improvements constitute the Wayō (Japanese style). Later styles included the Great Buddha style (Daibutsuyō or Tenjikuyō), introduced to Japan by Priest Chōgen in the twelfth century, the Zen style (Zenshūyō or Karayō), also introduced in the twelfth century, and the eclectic style (Secchūyō), which combined features of the previous three styles.

History of Hōryūji

Founded by Prince Shōtoku, Hōryūji was built in 607, burned in 670, and rebuilt a few years later (date uncertain). In the original

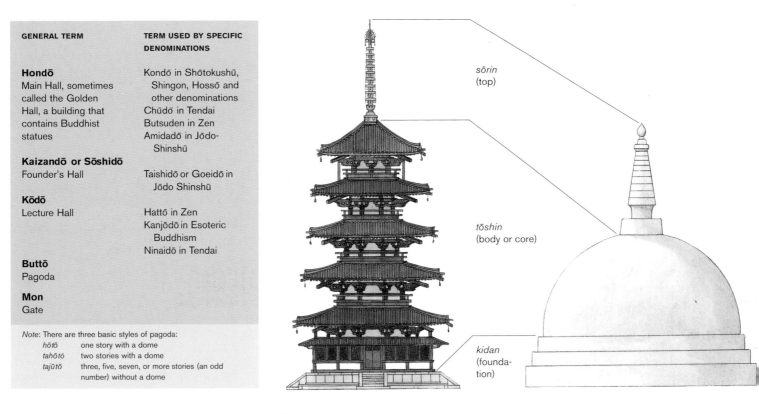

GENERAL TERM	TERM USED BY SPECIFIC DENOMINATIONS
Hondō Main Hall, sometimes called the Golden Hall, a building that contains Buddhist statues	Kondō in Shōtokushū, Shingon, Hossō and other denominations Chūdō in Tendai Butsuden in Zen Amidadō in Jōdo-Shinshū
Kaizandō or Sōshidō Founder's Hall	Taishidō or Goeidō in Jōdo Shinshū
Kōdō Lecture Hall	Hattō in Zen Kanjōdō in Esoteric Buddhism Ninaidō in Tendai
Buttō Pagoda	
Mon Gate	

Note: There are three basic styles of pagoda:
hōtō	one story with a dome
tahōtō	two stories with a dome
tajūtō	three, five, seven, or more stories (an odd number) without a dome

sōrin (top)

tōshin (body or core)

kidan (foundation)

Above: Comparison between the pagoda and the Indian stupa, from which the pagoda evolved.

Below: The south gate, pagoda, and Main Hall of Hōryūji Temple.

compound, the Main Hall was lined up behind the pagoda, as at Shitennōji (page 39), breaking the symmetry of the original layout. When Hōryūji was rebuilt, the pagoda was placed to the left of the Main Hall.

Hōryūji consists of a Western Precinct, where the main buildings are located, and an Eastern Precinct, containing the Yume-dono (Hall of Dreams), built in 739 for the repose of the soul of Prince Shōtoku, and the Denpōdō, built by Prince Shōtoku's wife for her home. The latter is a valuable example of an aristocratic dwelling from the Nara Period. Other buildings were added over the years.

Western Precinct

The Western Precinct of Hōryūji consists of the inner gate, the pagoda and Main Hall, and the Lecture Hall to the rear. The Main Hall is a two-story building, nine bays in width. A central space (*moya*), three bays wide by two deep, houses the altar with its images. Both the pagoda and the Main Hall have pent roofs midway on the first floor, giving the appearance of an additional story. The pent roofs cover outer aisles (*hisashi*), added in the Nara Period to provide more space. The projection of the eaves in the five-story pagoda, as well as the area and height of the floors, is graduated to produce a tapered effect that provides a sense of grace and stability. The buildings are constructed of *hinoki* (Japanese cypress).

Nara Period Temples

When the capital was moved to Heijōkyō in 710, most Buddhist denominations followed. In addition to the seven great temples of Nara, supported by the State, many private temples were constructed by aristocrats. Compared to the architecture of the preceding period, Nara Period temples, influenced by the Tang Dynasty of China, were on a grander scale.

State Sponsored Temples

The Emperor Shōmu, an ardent advocate of Buddhism, established Tōdaiji as the headquarters of a national system of monasteries (*kokubunji*) and nunneries (*kokubunniji*). Tōdaiji housed a great bronze Buddha, 17 meters high, that involved nearly 10 percent of the population in its construction and required around 1,665,000 man days to complete. In the year 752, 10,000 priests and dignitaries from many parts of Asia, and as far away as Persia, assembled in Nara to attend the eye-opening ceremony, during which a famous Indian priest painted in the eyes of the Great Buddha (Daibutsu). This ceremony was intended to symbolize the fact that Buddhism had become firmly established in Japan and that the Land of the Rising Sun was now a nation ready to make its own contribution to Asian culture and politics.

Heijōkyō was the headquarters of the seven great National Temples of Nara: Hōryūji (rebuilt no later than 710), Kōfukuji (moved from Asuka in 710), Daianji (called Daikandaiji when it was moved to Heijōkyō in 710 and renamed Daianji in 745), Gangōji (moved from Asuka in 718), Yakushiji (moved from Fujiwarakyō in 718), Tōdaiji (inaugurated in 752), and Saidaiji (constructed in 765). Some of these national temples were the headquar-

Above: The West Pagoda of Yakushiji Temple is a recent reproduction of a Nara Period temple. It was reconstructed on the site of an original pagoda dating to around 730.

Opposite: The bell tower with a tile roof at Tōdaiji Temple in Nara. Rebuilt in the Kamakura Period, the tower houses a bell dating to 752. Both the tower and bell are National Treasures.

Right: The Sangatsudō, on the grounds of Tōdaiji, consists of two early buildings covered by a common roof (the Narabidō or "side-by-side" style). Although lacking the symmetry of classic temples, the overall effect is pleasing.

ters of the six main denominations imported from China, known collectively as the Six Sects of Nara. All six denominations advocated highly abstract metaphysical philosophies that failed to gain popularity in Japan. As a consequence, most never actually established themselves as independent denominations.

Next to Tōdaiji, the most important of the

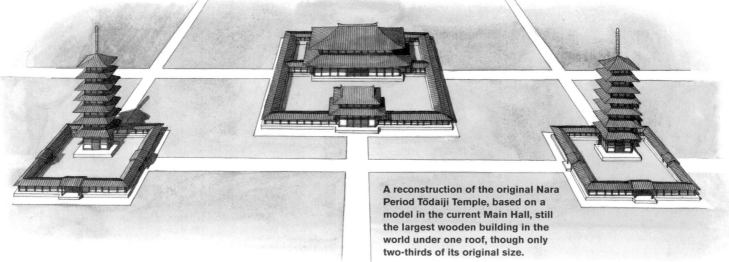

A reconstruction of the original Nara Period Tōdaiji Temple, based on a model in the current Main Hall, still the largest wooden building in the world under one roof, though only two-thirds of its original size.

by the Emperor Shōmu to teach the Buddhist precepts in Japan. Ganjin accepted the invitation but it took him six attempts to cross the ocean. During the twelve years involved in this effort, many of his disciples perished at sea and Ganjin lost his eyesight. He arrived in Nara in 754, totally blind. He assumed a post at Tōdaiji, where he provided Buddhist instruction for the retired Emperor Shōmu and the reigning Empress Kōken. Ganjin resigned from Tōdaiji in 759 to build Tōshōdaiji, where he remained until his death four years later. Two of the original buildings at Tōshōdaiji, the Main Hall and the Lecture Hall, remain today, making Tōshōdaiji the most important early Buddhist architectural site in Japan, apart from Hōryūji.

Left: Pagodas at Yakushiji Temple, Nara. Two pagodas were built in the early eighth century in the Hakuhō style. One burned and has only recently been rebuilt. The pagodas are unusual in that they appear to have six stories. In reality, there are three stories with intermediate eaves (*mokoshi*). The original pagoda, in the foreground, is one of the few remaining structures from the Nara Period.

Evolution of Temple Styles

Between the founding of Asukadera Temple in 596 and the inauguration of Tōdaiji Temple in 752, there were several significant changes in Buddhist architecture and temple layout. First, there was an increase in the size of the Main Hall and the pagoda. Second, the pagoda was moved to a more peripheral location. Third, there was an increase in the complexity of the roof bracketing system, as roofs grew larger and heavier.

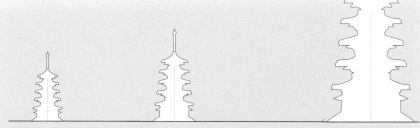

Hōryūji Pagoda   Yakushiji Pagoda   Tōdaiji Pagoda

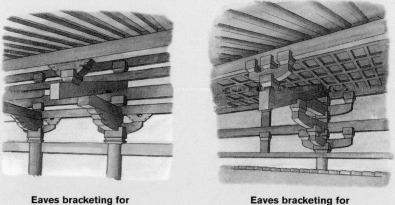

Eaves bracketing for the Hōryūji Main Hall.

Eaves bracketing for the Yakushiji Pagoda.

seven great temples of Nara was Gangōji, discussed previously. Originally called Hōkōji, the temple was renamed Gangōji when it was moved to Nara. It quickly became a center for the reception of new ideas from China and the propagation of Buddhist thought in Japan. In accordance with a government ranking system instituted in 749, Gangōji received 2,000 *chōbu* of land, second only to Tōdaiji, which received 4,000. Yakushiji, Kōfukuji, and Daianji each received 1,000 *chobu*, and Hōryūji received 500. One *chōbu* consists of approximately 39,600 hectares of farmland, whose purpose was to provide income for support of a temple. Saidaiji was not built until 764 and thus was not a recipient of this initial patronage.

Another Nara temple of great importance, but not one of the State-supported institutions mentioned above, is Tōshōdaiji. The founder, the great Chinese priest Ganjin, was invited

Post-Buddhist Shinto Shrines

When Buddhism was officially adopted as the State religion in the seventh century, indigenous beliefs, practices, and material culture associated with the Way of the Gods became known as Shinto. Shinto shrines could not help but be influenced by the powerful new religion. Major introductions to Shinto architecture included curved roofs, vermilion colored wood, metal ornamentation, and special spaces for worshippers.

Shrine Classification

Shrines can be classified into four categories depending upon the type of Main Hall (or lack thereof), where a sacred object representing the *kami* (deity) of the shrine is housed. The first, and most basic type, are shrines without any Main Hall. The *kami* worshipped at this type of shrine resides in a natural object and thus needs no artificial domicile. The second category consists of the Pre-Buddhist styles discussed earlier, such as the Sumiyoshi, Izumo, and Shimmei styles.

The third category consists of styles that originated after the introduction of Buddhism and thus were heavily influenced by Buddhist architecture. Examples are the Kasuga style (exemplified by Kasuga Shrine in Nara), Nagare style (exemplified by Ujigami Shrine in Uji), Hie style (exemplified by Hiyoshi Shrine in Shiga Perfecture), and Hachiman style (exemplified by Usa Jingū in Oita Perfecture).

The fourth category is known as Gūji, a combination of shrine and temple where a deified person is worshipped. The first such shrine was Kitano Tenmangū in Kyoto City, built in 947 to pacify the spirit of Sugawara Michizane, a court noble who was wrongly accused by his enemies and subsequently exiled to Kyushu. Another example is Nikkō Tōshōgū where Tokugawa Ieyasu, the first Tokugawa shogun, is worshipped as the guardian of the Kanto Plain.

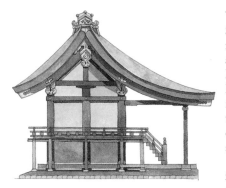

Above: Nagare style, the most common type of post-Buddhist shrine. The entrance is on the long side, as in the Shimmei style, but the roof is extended over the steps to provide shelter for worshippers. The building in the photograph on the right is Ujigami Shrine at Uji, near Kyoto.

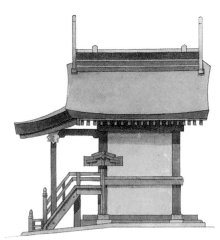

Below: Kasuga style, the second most common type of shrine. The entrance is on the end, but a separate roof covers the steps. The buildings shown below right at Enjōji Temple in Nara Prefecture were moved from Kasuga Shrine in Nara at the beginning of the thirteenth century when Kasuga Shrine was remodeled.

Evolution of Shrine Styles

The earliest sacred spaces were cleared patches in the forest or on the beach, covered with white gravel, prepared for the "descent" of the *kami*. Even today, there are numerous locations, often associated with fertility or food, that are considered to be the domicile of *kami*. Sacred spots are associated with natural features. For example, when walking through the mountains, it is not uncommon to see caves where rocks have been piled up to honor the *kami*. Other sacred spots include mountains, waterfalls, unusual trees, and islands. Especially important are mountains, such as Mount Fuji, since mountains are closer to the sky and thus serve as convenient "landing places" for sky deities. Sacred locations are marked by a rope or a Shinto gate (*torii*). They require no buildings to function as places of worship.

The earliest shrine buildings were associated with specific clans and were modeled after the living quarters of a chief (such as at Izumo) or elevated storehouses (such as at Ise). The main building was the Honden, which enshrined a specific *kami* symbolized by a sacred object such as a sword, jewel, or mirror. No special provisions were provided for worshippers, who usually could not enter the most sacred areas of the shrine grounds.

After the introduction of Buddhism, the idea of a temple, where members of a congregation could assemble to worship and participate in ceremonies, inspired Shinto shrines to construct special areas for worshippers. This was done by extending the roof of the Honden or building a separate worship hall (the Haiden). Gradually, other buildings were added, such as a stage for sacred performances.

Eventually, Shinto beliefs and practices became widely established among the common people and shrines were built in every village and town to enshrine a protector deity for the

ELEMENTS COMMON TO ALL SHRINES, EXCEPT THE FIRST TYPE

Term	Explanation
sandō	Approach to the shrine, lined with trees or lanterns.
torii	Shinto gate.
kaki	Fence, wall, or corridor used to distinguish a sacred area from the outside world.
shimenawa	Rope representing *kekkai*, the line between purity and impurity.
suibansha	Basin containing water for ritual purification of mouth and hands before entering the shrine grounds.
komainu, shishi	Statues of lions or lion dogs that guard a shrine.
honden	Main Hall, or *kami* hall, where the *kami* is enshrined. Cannot be entered by lay people.
haiden	Worship Hall where individuals pray and services are conducted.

Note: Some types of shrine have *chigi* (crossed finials) and *katsuogi* (poles placed across the ridge to help hold the ridge cover down). The number of *katsuogi* on the roof indicates the status of the shrine – the greater the number of *katsuogi*, the higher the status of the shrine.

residents. Even individual houses had household shrines – a main Shinto shelf (*kamidana*) for holding ritual objects, and special shrines for particular parts of the house, such as a shrine for the god of the hearth and a shrine for the god of the kitchen. On ceremonial occasions, such as a rice planting or harvesting festival, the local deity would be moved from the village shrine in a portable shrine to rice fields in the neighborhood of the village for a special ceremony, after which it was moved back to the permanent shrine building.

Because Shinto was so closely associated with the surroundings and activities of everyday life, it came to play an important role in the Japanese psyche, with its tendency to give precedence to the immediate, direct experience of nature over the lofty philosophical and ethical precepts of Buddhism.

Nevertheless, in many cases Shinto and Buddhist beliefs and practices were amalgamated into a syncretic shrine/temple, some of which can still be seen today. With the growth of State Shinto, many sought to elevate Shintoism over Buddhism, with the consequence that after the Meiji Restoration of 1868, shrines and temples were separated. All shrines were required to join a national association, with Ise Shrine as the head. This new organization, dedicated to the glory of the Emperor and the Japanese State, built many new shrines, known as *jingū* rather than the normal *jinja*, in the Shimmei style. These shrines, such as the Meiji Shrine in Tokyo and Kashihara Jingū in Nara Prefecture, were built on a grand scale. After World War II, State Shinto was abolished.

Above: Kashihara Jingū, an example of State Shinto architecture, with its stately buildings, covered corridors, and large graveled area, reminiscent of the Imperial Palace in Kyoto. Kashihara Jingū is dedicated to the legendary first emperor, Jimmu, whose tomb mound is nearby.

Below: Gate to Kamigano Shrine in Kyoto City. The influence of Buddhist temples is apparent in the multi-story gate and the covered corridors.

Right: Usa Jingū in Oita Prefecture, originally built in 725, is the most important of the numerous shrines in Japan dedicated to the mythical Emperor Ōjin, his mother, Empress Jingū, and Ōjin's consort, Hime-Ōkami – three deities identified with Hachiman, the Shinto god of war. The Honden of Usa Jingū is a classic example of the Hachiman style, with its adjacent, connected structures. Shown here is the Nanchū Rōmon (entrance gate), built in 1743 and repaired in 1941. The gate is reserved for the use of imperial emissaries. See page 20 for a discussion of the *rōmon* gate style (two stories with one roof).

Developing a Cultural Identity

The Heian Period (794–1185) began when the capital was moved from Heijōkyō (Nara) to Heiankyō (present-day Kyoto), partly to escape the influence of powerful Buddhist temples in the former capital. The culture of Tang China continued to dominate for a time, but Japan eventually reduced contact with the continent and assimilated what it had learned, to produce a distinctive culture of its own.

1 Heiankyō (Kyoto)
2 Enryakuji Temple (Mount Hiei)
3 Lake Biwa
4 Onjōji Temple (Ōtsu)
5 Byōdōin Temple (Uji)
6 Heijōkyō (Nara)
7 Jōruriji Temple
8 Murōji Temple (Nara)
9 Tanzanjinja Shrine
10 Kinpusenji Temple (Mount Yoshino)
11 Kongōbuji Temple (Mount Kōya)
12 Kannonji Temple
13 Chūsonji Temple
14 Usa Hachiman Shrine

The New Capital

The capital was moved from Heijōkyō (Nara) to Nagaokakyō in 784, and then to Heiankyō (Kyoto) in 794, where it remained for over a thousand years. Kyoto had all the requirements, according to Chinese principles of geomancy, for a paradise on earth: a river (Kamogawa River) on the east (home of Seiryū, dragon god) for providing pure drinking water; a road (Sanyōdō Road) on the west (home of Byakko, white tiger god) for bringing in food; a body of water (Ogura Pond) to the south (home of Suzaku, vermilion phoenix god) to provide unobstructed access to sunshine; and a mountain (Mount Funaoka) to the north (home of Genbu, snake god curled around a turtle) for protection. Paintings of these four gods have been found in ancient tomb mounds. This basic system was used not only for selecting capital sites, but for choosing castle sites, beginning in the Momoyama Period (1573–1600).

The design of the new capital was similar to that of Heijōkyō. It was laid out in a grid pattern, 5.5 kilometers from north to south and 4.7 kilometers from east to west, surrounded by a moat. In the north were the imperial palace grounds, in the vicinity of the present-day Nijō Castle. The palace grounds consisted of an enclosure about 1.4 kilometers by 1.2 kilometers, with 14 gates and several compounds, including the imperial residence,

residential apartments for family members and consorts, ceremonial halls, and the imperial halls of state. The main gate opened onto a wide thoroughfare, Suzaku Ōji, the same name used for the central street at Heijōkyō. This street connected the palace with the city's main entrance to the south, the Rajōmon Gate, which was flanked by Tōji Temple to the east and Saiji Temple to the west. Saiji no longer exists, but Tōji remains. Its pagoda, the largest in Japan, still dominates the landscape in that part of the city. Near the palace grounds were additional imperial residences, mansions belonging to the nobility, and government offices. The city also included other types of buildings such as Shinto shrines, market areas, and town houses (*machiya*) that served as residence-shops for artisans and retailers. According to one estimate, the capital had a population of around half a million people.

New Forms of Buddhism

In the early Heian Period, Saichō and Kūkai, two priests who had been studying in China, returned to Japan, bringing esoteric Buddhism with its emphasis upon the secret transmission of teachings. Its mystical beliefs and practices provided a powerful stimulus for the Buddhist art of the Heian Period, best known for its sculptures of Buddhist divinities, paintings, and mandalas (schematic pictorial diagrams of Buddhist divinities and cosmology). In the

Opposite: Byakkorō (White Tiger Tower) at Heian Shrine in Kyoto, one of a number of impressive structures at the shrine, which was constructed in 1895 to commemorate the 1,100th anniversary of moving the capital to Heiankyō (present-day Kyoto). The tower is linked by a covered corridor to the largest building, a two-thirds scale reproduction of the third Great Hall of State (Daigokuden), built in 1072 on the original palace grounds; the first Great Hall of State at Heiankyō burned in 876 and again in 1058.

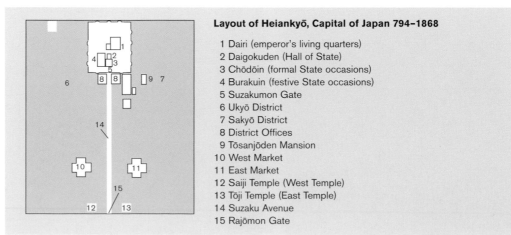

Layout of Heiankyō, Capital of Japan 794–1868

1 Dairi (emperor's living quarters)
2 Daigokuden (Hall of State)
3 Chōdōin (formal State occasions)
4 Burakuin (festive State occasions)
5 Suzakumon Gate
6 Ukyō District
7 Sakyō District
8 District Offices
9 Tōsanjōden Mansion
10 West Market
11 East Market
12 Saiji Temple (West Temple)
13 Tōji Temple (East Temple)
14 Suzaku Avenue
15 Rajōmon Gate

later Heian Period, Amida Buddhism was introduced from China. Amida Buddhism appealed to common people and aristocrats alike, with its promise that one could be reborn in Paradise simply by calling upon the name of Amida Buddha. Worshippers of Amida erected magnificent paradise halls designed to create an image of heaven on earth.

Flowering of indigenous Culture

The last half of the Heian Period is called the Fujiwara Epoch – a time when Japanese culture gradually developed its own distinctive

identity. This was facilitated by several factors, such as the suspension of official exchanges with China in the latter part of the ninth century. Another factor was that public lands, which had been taken by the Yamato Court in its bid to establish control over competing clans, increasingly fell into the hands of tax-free temples and the aristocracy. As taxes dried up, government bureaucracy ceased functioning and the court became isolated from the affairs of the country.

Members of the court spent their time in the pursuit of art, poetry, and romance. The highly refined culture of the period was expressed in the aesthetic ideals of *miyabi* (courtly elegance and tasteful refinement) and *mono no aware* (melancholy awareness of the transient beauty of nature). Indigenous cultural developments occurred in the areas of literature, facilitated by the invention of *kana*, a phonetic syllabary better suited to expressing Japanese sentiments than classical Chinese; Japanese style painting; and architecture. One of the most important developments in architecture was the maturation of Shinden style mansions (described below), originally developed in the Nara Period.

Roof Innovations

Urban temples in the Heian Period experimented with new methods of roofing with tile. In China, large tiled roofs were created by using a succession of thick, but short, overlapping rafters to create a long, curved rafter that rested directly on purlins (beams running at right angles to the rafters). Clay was added above the joints where the short rafters overlapped to reinforce the joints and to create a smooth, curved surface. This method proved to be unsuitable for Japan where heavy rains sometimes permeated the tiles to soak the clay. Since it took a long time for the clay to dry out, the moisture speeded the rot of the rafters. Another problem was that earthquakes tended to crack the clay.

The Japanese solved this problem by developing a double set of rafters, with thick weight-bearing cantilevers in between, that rested on purlins running at right angles to the rafters. Roof tiles rested on the upper set of rafters, referred to as "hidden rafters" because they could not be seen from the underside. Since the hidden rafters bore little of the weight of the tiles, they could be made from single long pieces of wood that were thin enough to be shaped into the desired curve.

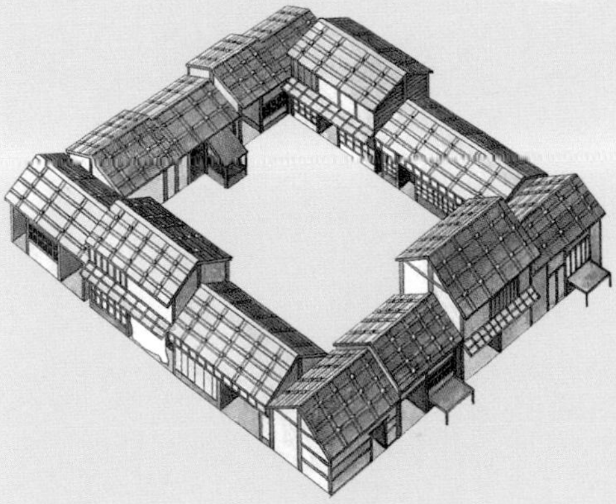

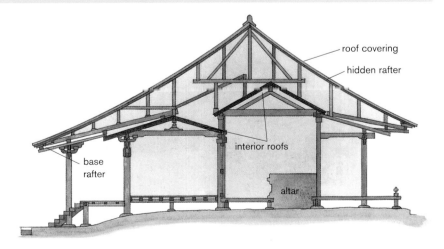

Left: A typical *machiya* **block (***chō***) was a compound with several** *machiya* **arranged around a common courtyard.**

Above: The work area, shown in the cutaway above, served as a passageway between the front and back doors. It contained the kitchen and provided storage for firewood and vegetables. Drawing based on a model at the National Museum of Japanese History.

Merchant Residence-Shops

There is little information about Heian Period *machiya* but a Muromachi Period screen at the National Museum of Japanese History, upon which the drawing above is based, indicates that they had board roofs weighted down with stones, and earthen floors divided into work areas and mat-covered living areas. The shop, adjacent to the street, had a raised platform where customers could sit.

This system not only eliminated the need for composite rafters and clay but also allowed the hidden rafters to be sloped at a different angle from the lower rafters (referred to as "base rafters") – in effect, creating a roof that had one appearance from the inside and another appearance from the outside. The new technique allowed considerable flexibility in terms of design. It also was a useful way of tying together two existing buildings or making it possible to create two distinct areas within a building, such as an inner and outer sanctum in Wayō style temples, where each has its own roof, but from the outside appears to have only a single roof.

roof covering

hidden rafter

interior roofs

base rafter

altar

Left: The large walled compound of Heian Shrine is entered through this majestic 24-meter-high two-story Ōtenmon Gate located to the south and in line with the Great Hall of State (Daigokuden) at the north end of the complex. Chinese influences are unmistakable in the vermilion posts, green tiled roofs, and white plastered walls of all the shrine buildings.

Palaces and Mansions

Heian Period Shinden style mansions featured a central hall (the *shinden*) connected to subsidiary buildings by long covered corridors. The entire walled complex, with its various courtyards, was arranged around a large garden consisting of a lake with an island reached by small bridges. Although none of these early mansions remain, the style influenced later palaces and temples, as well as residential architecture.

Architectural Features

The Shinden style originated in the Nara Period and achieved maturity in the late Heian Period. The basic features have been reconstructed from picture scrolls and archaeological excavations. The average lot size of mansions in the capital was one block (about 120 square meters), though a few, such as that of the powerful Fujiwara family that acted as regents for the emperor in the latter part of the Heian Period, occupied as much as two city blocks. The buildings of a Shinden style mansion were single-story structures consisting of a *moya* (main area) and *hisashi* (peripheral sections), raised on wooden posts sunk into the ground, and surrounded by wooden verandas reached by stairs. Floors and siding were unpainted wood and the roof was shingled or planked. To this point, there are obvious similarities to the indigenous taste represented by earlier structures such as prehistoric raised chiefs' houses. Other features, however, show the influence of continental principles, such as those used in Buddhist temples. For example, Shinden style mansions adopted a hipped-and-gable roof and the entire compound was surrounded by earthen walls with tiled roofs.

The fronts of the buildings in the compound consisted of hinged wooden shutters (*shitomido*) that allowed the upper half to be raised and the lower half to be removed when weather permitted. The inside was simple but elegant. There were few interior partitions and occupants sat on straw cushions, forerunners of the *tatami* mats of later residences, spread on wooden floors. Privacy was provided by paper sliding doors or folding screens, painted by the best-known artists of the day.

The *shinden* (main hall) was the residence of the head of the house, whereas subsidiary buildings were used by family members, consorts, and servants. The courtyard of the *shinden* provided the setting for special ceremonies and entertainment.

Kyoto Gosho

The original Imperial Palace in Kyoto, said to be the only major palace in the world made entirely of wood, was repeatedly damaged by fire. Following a fire in 1177, the Daigokuden (Great Hall of State) was not rebuilt. Originally, state ceremonies had all been carried out at the Daigokuden, but that function increasingly moved to the Shishinden (Ceremonial Hall). Over the next hundred years, the location of the palace was changed several times, often due to wars and fires. Instead of rebuilding, the *sato dairi* (town palace) system was developed whereby the residence of a high-ranking noble was taken over as the palace. All nobles above a certain rank were required to build a residence suitable for this purpose, in case it was needed in time of crisis, such as fire or war.

In 1331, the court settled upon the present palace site, about 2 kilometers east of the original palace compound, for a new palace. Like its predecessors, it was susceptible to repeated fires, with the result that nothing is left of the original buildings. In 1790, the palace was

Below: One of the scenes depicted in the picture scroll of Annual Rites and Ceremonies shows Tōsanjōden, the residence of the influential Fujiwara family in the Heian Period. Tōsanjōden, a fine example of a Shinden style mansion, occupied two city blocks north to south, surrounded by earth walls. The main building, the *shinden*, consisted of a central area, 4 by 11 meters, surrounded by verandas. Corridors connected the *shinden* to other buildings on the north, east, and west. On the south was a large garden used for ceremonies, as well as a pond, fed by a stream coming from higher ground on the northeast. Drawing based on a model at the National Museum of Japanese History.

rebuilt, based on historical research conducted by Uramatsu Kozen, in the original Heian Period style, though it reproduced only the domestic quarters of the original palace. No expense was spared to make the new palace a place of austere simplicity and quiet dignity – a symbol of imperial taste. In 1854, the palace was again partly destroyed by fire. The present compound was reconstructed in 1855 using the designs prepared for the previous palace.

The rectangular area of about 10.8 hectacres is enclosed by a tile-roofed earthen wall, approximately 455 meters long and 227 meters wide. Five white bands on the wall signify imperial status. Similar bands on the walls of temples or shrines indicate imperial patronage. The wall of the palace is transected by several major gates and 14 small emergency exits. The south gate is used only by the emperor and the east gate is used only by the empress or empress-dowager. The west wall contains three gates, one for court officials and the others for visitors. The north gate traditionally was reserved for imperial consorts and their ladies-in-waiting. The unlucky northeast corner, marked by a jog in the wall, is guarded by the carving of a monkey dressed as a Shinto priest.

Inside the compound are 18 buildings joined by covered corridors that create small Shinden style courtyards and gardens with streams, islands, bridges, rocks, and vegetation. The main structure is the Shishinden, a building used for ceremonial occasions. Like the main building of other Shinden style mansions, it has a high wooden floor and basically consists of a large, open central area with *hisashi* style pent roofs attached to the four sides. The building is enclosed by a veranda with a low railing. The magnificent roof of the Shishinden consists of a 30-centimeter-thick covering of cypress bark shingles. The 18 steps in front of the Shishinden represent the 18 court ranks allowed inside the palace. The Shishinden faces an enormous graveled courtyard where outdoor ceremonies and court dances were performed. Another building, the Seiryōden, was the living quarters for the emperor. In its center was an enclosed area, the Nurigome, which the emperor used for sleeping and for storing valuables.

The Imperial Palace moved to Tokyo at the beginning of the Meiji Period. After the move, the many residences of imperial relatives and court nobles that surrounded the palace were abandoned and gradually deteriorated.

Those areas were eventually transformed into the Kyoto Imperial Gardens, a beautifully planted area outside the walls of the palace and a quiet area for people living in Kyoto.

Today, the old Imperial Palace in Kyoto, while well maintained, is used only for the coronation of new emperors. An open house, when the general public can view the exteriors of many of the buildings, is held twice a year, once in the spring and once in the fall. Private visits can be arranged in advance with the Imperial Household Agency office located on the palace grounds.

Above: The Kogosho (meaning "small imperial palace") was mainly used as a ceremonial hall for crown princes. The architecture is transitional between the Shinden and Shoin styles. The building shown in this 1896 stone lithograph by Motoharu burned in 1954 and was rebuilt in 1958.

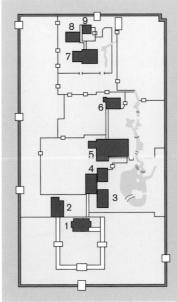

Simplified Layout of the Gosho
Reconstructed in 1855 after repeated fires, the present Imperial Palace in Kyoto is much smaller than the original, constructed in the Heian Period. Today, the palace is used only for the coronation of new emperors.

1 Shishinden (Hall of State)
2 Seiryōden (originally the private residence of the emperor, later used as a ceremony hall)
3 Kogosho (small imperial palace)
4 Ogakumonjo (study hall)
5 Otsunegoten (residence for the emperor)
6 Ohanagoten (residence for the crown prince)
7 Kōgō Otsunegoten (unofficial residence for the empress)
8 Wakamiyagoten and Himemiyagoten (residences for the royal children)
9 Higyōsha (official residence for the empress)

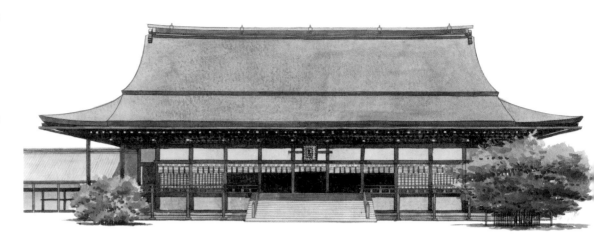

Influence upon Subsequent Architecture

Although there are no extant early Shinden style mansions, the Shinden style had an important influence, not only on the Kyoto Imperial Palace, but on many other forms of architecture, including samurai mansions of the Kamakura Period, palace temples of the Muromachi Period (such as Kinkakuji, Temple of the Golden Pavilion in Kyoto), and some Edo Period Buddhist temple compounds (such as Ninnaji Temple in Kyoto and Enmanin Temple, part of the Onjōji Temple complex in Ōtsu, Shiga Prefecture). Perhaps most important, however, was the influence of the Shinden style upon the Shoin style used in detached palaces of the Edo Period, such as Katsura Rikyū in Kyoto – the forerunner of early modern residential architecture.

A feature of the Shinden style that had a major influence upon subsequent architecture was the large, open central space (*moya*) surrounded by peripheral sections (*hisashi*). This, plus the use of movable room dividers rather than permanent interior walls, provided considerable flexibility in that interior space could be divided in different ways depending upon the occasion.

Other important features of the Shinden style were raised wooden floors (*takayuka*) and shingled roofs. These features distinguish palace and residential architecture from that of Chinese style Buddhist temples, which had tile roofs and were constructed on platforms made of rocks and tamped earth. As a result, subsequent architecture had a lighter feeling, a characteristic that was incorporated and further developed in the residential architecture of ordinary people.

Mountain Temples

Right: The first building constructed at Enryakuji was the Konponchūdō. Situated on the spot where Saichō built a meditation hut in 788, before his trip to China, the Konponchūdō was small (about 9 meters wide) with a cypress bark roof. The building was eventually expanded to encompass two sections: an outer part (*raidō* or *gejin*) for the worshippers, and a sunken inner part (*naijin*) containing an altar and the main images. The *naijin* has a stone floor 3 meters lower than the wooden floor of the *raidō*. Destroyed in 1571 by Oda Nobunaga, the Konponchūdō was rebuilt in 1642.

Below: Moved from Onjōji Temple in 1595 after the Mount Hiei complex was destroyed in 1571, the Shakadō is the Main Hall of the Western Precinct at Enryakuji Temple on Mount Hiei, near Kyoto. Though Chinese in inspiration, its wood shingles and mountain setting give it a Japanese feeling.

The esoteric Buddhist denominations of the Heian Period, Tendai and Shingon, built many of their temples in the mountains to provide a quiet place for study and meditation. This was a departure from the predominantly ceremonial function of the great Chinese style monasteries of Nara. The mountain setting required a departure in other ways as well, such as abandoning the symmetrical layout and the enclosing walls of earlier urban temples.

Influence of Indigenous Taste

As discussed earlier, Chinese and Korean culture had an enormous impact upon Japan. Buddhism, with its sophisticated philosophy and advanced architectural techniques, was eagerly accepted by the Japanese educated classes in the Asuka and Nara Periods. Nevertheless, indigenous standards of taste, exemplified in the Ise shrines, began to influence Buddhist temples, beginning with Hōryūji in the Asuka Period and reaching maturity in the mountain temples of the Heian Period. The influence of these indigenous standards of taste upon mountain temples can be summarized as follows:

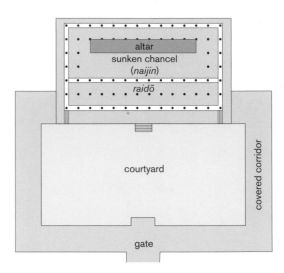

- an irregular ground plan due to the uneven terrain, resulting in an asymmetrical arrangement of buildings;
- greater use of natural materials, such as cypress bark, rather than tile, on roofs;
- greater sensitivity to the natural surroundings, such as placing buildings among the trees rather than clearing the vegetation;

Previous page: Three-storied pagoda of Seigantoji, a seventh-century Tendai temple located near the 113-meter-high Nachi Falls, one of the most sacred spots in Shinto. Located in Wakayama Prefecture, Seigantoji is the starting point of a 33-temple pilgrimage of temples on the Kii Peninsula dedicated to Kannon, goddess of mercy.

Below: The Tahōtō style pagoda ("many jeweled pagoda") was created for the Tendai and Shingon sects of Buddhism. The hemispherical area on the first floor, which has some resemblance to the original Indian stupa from which pagodas were derived, is enclosed by subsidiary sections with pent roofs (mokoshi) on four sides, thus creating a square floor area. The pagoda shown here is at Ishiyamadera Temple in Shiga Prefecture.

■ a preference for buildings that generally were more delicate in feeling than Chinese style temples with their massive tiled roofs.

Good examples of esoteric mountain temples from the Heian Period are Enryakuji Temple on Mount Hiei, near Kyoto; Kongōbuji Temple on Mount Kōya, near the present city of Wakayama; and Murōji Temple, located in a beautiful mountainous area south of Nara.

Mount Hiei

In 804, Saichō was sent by the emperor to a renowned monastery in China, located on the sacred mountain of T'ien-t'ai, to study the teachings of a school of Buddhism that was based upon the Lotus Sutra (a scripture from India) but that was also influenced by Chinese Taoism. Tendai, as it was called in Japan, taught that the absolute is inherent in all phenomena and that enlightenment comes from a combination of studying the scriptures, religious practice, and meditation. When he returned from China, Saichō's Tendai Lotus Sect was added to the list of the six Nara sects officially recognized by the government and provided with State support.

Saichō, posthumously known as Dengyō Daishi, established the headquarters of Tendai Buddhism – Enryakuji Temple – on Mount Hiei, to the northeast of Kyoto, to guard Kyoto's unlucky direction. Enryakuji has long been the most influential Buddhist seminary in Japan, having trained the founders of the Jōdo, Jōdo Shin, Nichiren, Sōtō, and Rinzai Zen sects, among others. At its height, Enryakuji encompassed around 300 temples. It became so powerful that thousands of its "warrior monks" raided Kyoto on various occasions to exercise political influence on the capital. In 1571, Oda Nobunaga, the first of the three great generals to unify Japan in the Momoyama Period (1573–1600), destroyed Enryakuji and massacred nearly everyone on the sacred mountain. Today, the much reduced Enryakuji consists of around 30 buildings, organized into three precincts: the Tōdō, Saitō, and Yokawa.

Mount Kōya

When Kūkai (posthumously known as Kōbō Daishi) was studying in China, he was most influenced by a form of Buddhism in which Maha-Vairocana (Dainichi Nyorai in Japanese) is the cosmic Buddha from which all other Buddhas emanate. There are four main emanations that correspond to the four cardinal directions. The most important of these emanations for later developments in Japanese Buddhism is Amida, the Lord of Boundless Light (Buddha of the West). For some later sects, Amida became the paramount deity who resides in the Western Paradise.

When Kūkai returned from China, he established dual headquarters at Tōji Temple in Kyoto and at Kongōbuji Temple on Mount

Kōya, Kūkai called the new denomination Shingon (meaning "True Word"). Shingon, known as "mystical Buddhism" because its esoteric doctrines cannot be explained in words, attaches great importance to the ritual incantation of mantras, formulae that symbolically represent the nature and structure of the universe. Today, the original 1,000 or so temples at the headquarters on Mount Kōya have been reduced to 123, and very little of the original complex remains.

The Architecture of Esoteric Buddhism

The esoteric denominations emphasized the gradual initiation of believers into secret knowledge and ritual practices. In accordance with this emphasis, the Main Hall was divided into two distinct areas, an outer area for novices and an inner sanctum for the initiated. The inner area contains an altar, with space behind it for additional images. The inner and outer areas, each with its own roof, were united by a hipped-and-gable roof that covered

Above: Kongōbuji Temple on Mount Kōya, near the present city of Wakayama, is an example of a Shingon Buddhist mountain temple from the Heian period. Set on a high plateau among towering evergreen forests, it is a peaceful place for study and contemplation.

both roof structures, employing the double roof system described earlier. A raised wooden floor replaced the tile or stone floor of earlier temples, the eaves were extended to cover the wooden steps of the front entry by the use of cantilevers, and shingles or bark often replaced tile. Finally, as mentioned above, an emphasis upon the symmetrical arrangement of buildings was replaced by a preference for adapting the layout of the buildings to the natural setting. This modified Tang style architecture gradually came to be known in later periods as the Wayō (Japanese) style to distinguish it from new styles that were being imported from China.

Murōji

At the end of the Nara Period, Murōji was remodeled and attached to Kōfukuji Temple in Nara. In 1694, it became an independent Shingon temple. Until recently, nearby Mount Kōya, headquarters of the Shingon sect, was

Layout of Murōji

1 Five-story Pagoda
2 Hondō (first Main Hall)
3 Kondō (second Main Hall)

Left: The Kondō (second Main Hall) at Murōji, built in the early Heian Period, has a hipped shingled roof and is accommodated to the slope on which it is built by a stone terrace that supports the wooden veranda. The natural cypress forest can be seen in the background.

closed to women. To provide an opportunity for women to follow the Shingon faith, Kūkai, the founder of Shingon Buddhism, decreed that Murōji, a typical early mountain temple, should be open to females. For that reason, Murōji has another name, "Nyonin Koya," meaning "Mount Koya for Women." Unlike the great temples of Nara, the buildings, scattered up the slope of a mountain, were constructed wherever relatively flat spots could be found. The concept of a clearly demarcated compound surrounded by a wall was abandoned, and much of the natural forest setting was preserved.

The most important buildings at Murōji are the Kondō, the Hondō, the five-storied pagoda, and the Miedō (inner sanctuary), where Kūkai is enshrined. Dating from the Heian Period, the Kondō houses several important images. The front part, supported on stilts, was added in the Edo Period as an outer sanctuary (*gejin*). The Hondō, dating from the Kamakura Period, houses a statue of Nyoirin Kannon. The pagoda, one of the smallest and most elegant in Japan, was recently restored after being severely damaged by a typhoon. Beyond the pagoda are 400 steps leading to the Miedō. The bark-covered roofs and natural wood blend unobtrusively into the forest, providing a good example of native sentiment in Buddhist architecture.

Above: The weathering paint on the exterior of the Kondō creates a patina of age, which is favored by many Japanese.

Left: Built in the Wayō style, the 16-meter, five-story pagoda at Murōji is the smallest in Japan. It is also one of the most beautiful.

Paradise Halls

Above: The three-story pagoda (restored in the Kamakura Period) situated across the pond from the Amida Hall at Jōruriji.

According to an ancient Buddhist prophecy, the world would enter into *mappō* (a dark period), beginning in 1052, during which it would be impossible to attain enlightenment by good works, meditation, and ceremonies. The only way to salvation would be through personal faith in Amida Buddha. By the late Heian Period, "paradise halls" dedicated to Amida Buddha were being built all over Japan.

Background of the Prophecy

Mappō means "the latter end of the law" (*dharma*), a time beginning 1,500 years after the death of the historical Buddha, when his teaching would lose its power and society would become degenerate. The Heian Period appeared to fit the prophecy. Degeneracy seemed to be everywhere, extending even to Buddhist monasteries where monks often appeared to be more interested in wealth, power, and pleasure than in spiritual values. The monk Kūya traveled about Japan preaching about the glories of heaven and the horrors of hell, and the monk Genshin expounded upon the worship of Amida Buddha, the Buddha of Boundless Light, who would ensure the rebirth in Jōdo, the Pure Land, of anyone who called upon his name in an act of sincere faith. Basically this involved the practice of *nembutsu*, repeating the name of Amida Buddha in the formula Namu Amida Butsu, meaning "Homage to Amida Buddha."

This emphasis upon grace rather than self-effort set the stage for the development, in later periods, of various denominations of Pure Land Buddhism, the first of which was Jōdo-shū, founded by Hōnen Shōnin (1133–1212). The headquarters of Jōdo-shū is Chionin Temple in Kyoto, founded in 1234. Hōnen's chief disciple was Shinran Shōnin (1173–1262), founder of Jōdo Shinshū (True Sect of Jōdo). The teachings of Kūya and Genshin caught on and court nobles began to build private paradise halls on their estates, situated on a garden and pond, in the manner of Shinden style mansions. The goal was to create visions of the Pure Land (the Western Paradise) on earth. These teachings spread to rural areas, where powerful families built Amida Halls like those in Kyoto.

Jōruriji

Jōruriji Temple, in Kyoto Prefecture, consists of a pond with a three-tiered pagoda rising from a dense forest on the east side and a paradise hall on the west. The pagoda, moved from a temple in Kyoto in 1178, represents the Eastern Paradise of Yakushi Nyorai (the Buddha of healing), whose image it houses. The oblong paradise hall, built in 1107 but dismantled and moved to its present location in 1157, represents Amida Buddha's Western Paradise. It houses nine statues of Amida, each representing one of the nine stages of Nirvana. There is a small island in the middle of the pond that represents the present world, halfway between the Eastern and Western paradises. This combination of symbolism and natural beauty evokes a mystical realm that can transport the believer into an experience of heaven on earth. Building paradise halls with nine Amida Buddhas was common in the latter part of the Heian Period, but Jōruriji is the only one of its type left.

Layout of Jōruriji

1 Amida Hall
2 Three-story Pagoda

Left: Earth, represented by an island, is situated between the Western Paradise, represented by the Amida Hall, and the Eastern Paradise, represented by the pagoda on the other side of the pond.

Below: The Amida Hall at Jōruriji is situated so that worshippers standing on the east bank of the pond can face west towards the nine statues of Amida Buddha housed in the hall, each representing one of the nine stages of Nirvana.

Right: Layout of Byōdōin, shaped like a phoenix, with the central hall in the middle and covered corridors on both sides and to the rear.

Byōdōin

In 1052, Fujiwara-no-Yorimichi, the son of the powerful regent Fujiwara Michinaga, turned one of his family villas, at Uji, south of Kyoto, into a temple known as Byōdōin, and in the following year he began work on Hōōdō (Phoenix Hall), a paradise hall dedicated to the worship of Amida. While fires, earthquakes and floods, even civil wars, left the hall in peace, the other buildings were burned in 1336 by Kusunoki Masashige, a follower of Emperor Go-Daigo, who mounted a failed rebellion against the Kamakura shogunate. Today, only the Hōōdō, the oldest and best example of a paradise hall, and the Kannondō (dedicated to Kannon, goddess of mercy) remain from the original temple compound.

The structure of the Phoenix Hall, the central building of the temple, is elegantly designed to represent the image of a many-storied building, as depicted in sutras. It resembles a stylized phoenix, with wing-like corridors on both sides bearing gabled roofs and raised eaves and a tail corridor to the rear. The pair of phoenixes mounted on top of the central roofline are National Treasures.

The Phoenix Hall houses an eleventh-century, 3-meter-high gilded statue of Amida (another National Treasure) meditating on a lotus throne beneath a lavish canopy, surrounded by delicate woodcarvings of worshipping Bodhisattvas making music, holding Buddhist artifacts, or praying.

The Phoenix Hall is situated to the west of Ajiike Pond. Members of the Fujiwara family would sit on the other side of the pond gazing at the beautiful Amida Hall and imagining their rebirth in the Western Paradise.

Above: Phoenix Hall (Hōōdō) at Byōdōin. The gentle curves of the roof were made possible by the double roof construction method, discussed earlier. The overall effect was further softened by beveling the posts, eave brackets, and rafters. The original red coloring of the wood and the lavish interior decorations have become greatly subdued by time. Restoration of the interior to its original condition is underway.

Above: The Konjikidō Amida Hall at Chūsonji Temple, a National Treasure, is one of two surviving structures from the Heian Period at a complex that originally comprised over 40 buildings. Built in 1124, the interior of the gold-plated hall stands in stark contrast to what can be seen from outside – an earthquake- and fire-resistant reinforced concrete Sheath Hall built in 1970. The other surviving structure is the Sutra Hall (Kyōzō), built in 1108. The complex is situated in a grove of ancient cedars.

Chūsonji

One of the few remaining paradise halls from the Heian Period is the Konjikidō of the hilltop Chūsonji, a ninth-century temple founded by priest Ennin in Hiraizumi in Iwate Prefecture, northern Japan, which began as a military outpost.

Fujiwara-no-Kiyohira, leader of the northern branch of the Fujiwara family, decided to make Hiraizumi his capital, and modeled it after Kyoto. He rebuilt Chūsonji, including over 40 buildings and pagodas. Of these, only the Konjikidō and Kyōzō (sutra hall) remain. The Konjikidō is a small Amida Hall (18 meters square) dating from 1124. Its entire surface is gilded with gold, giving rise to its popular name, Golden Hall. Though small, the Golden Hall houses three Amida trinities, flanked by statues of six Jisō boddhisatvas and four guardian kings. Beneath the hall are interred the mummies of the first three Fujiwara lords. The Golden Hall was restored in 1962, at which time it was enclosed by a fireproof building shown above. Nearby is the Kyu Oidō, a wooden hall built in 1288, which protected the Konjikido for 680 years. The Golden Hall of Chusonji is considered to be one of the finest examples of craftsmanship from the Heian Period. Its location in northern Japan makes it even more unique.

More Recent Paradise Halls

Nishi Honganji Temple, headquarters of the original Jōdo Shinshū denomination founded by Shinran, began as a mausoleum erected in honor of Shinran by his daughter. In 1591, Toyotomi Hideyoshi granted the temple a tract of land near the present Kyoto Station.

The original buildings constructed at this site were burned in 1617 by monks from Enryakuji Temple on Mount Hiei. The Founder's Hall was reconstructed in 1636 and the restored Amida Hall was completed in 1760. Both are classified as Important Cultural Assets. Most of the temple complex has been designated a World Cultural Heritage Site.

Two Noh stages, the Hiunkaku Flying Cloud Pavilion (which, together with Kinkakuji and Ginkakuji, is one of the three most famous pavilions in Japan), and the great Karamon Gate are thought to have come from Hideyoshi's Fushimi Castle, which was dismantled by Tokugawa Ieyasu. The Karamon Gate is a good example of the ornate qualities favored in the Momoyama Period.

Also on the grounds is the largest extant Shoin style building (see page 81), which includes several lavishly decorated rooms, used by the abbot for relaxing and entertaining important guests. In contrast to the magnificence of the Shoin, is the more subtle Kuro Shoin (Black Study).

Today there are two Honganji temples in Kyoto: the original temple, described above, popularly known as Nishi Honganji (West Honganji), and Higashi Honganji (East Honganji), which was established nearby in 1602, with the encouragement of the shogun Tokugawa Ieyasu, who feared the immense power of the original sect. Despite the schism, Nishi Honganji is the headquarters for 10,500 temples in Japan and throughout the world.

Above right: The Amida Hall at Nishi Honganji in Kyoto measures 37 by 42 meters, and has a height of 29 meters. The building has a large *gejin* (area for the congregation) to accommodate the many lay people who come here to worship.

Center: Inside the Amida Hall is a statue of Amida Buddha on the altar, flanked by portraits of the Seven Patriarchs from India, China, and Japan. The woodwork in the *gejin* is unpainted while the *naijin* (altar area) is decorated with gold leaf, black lacquer, and multiple colors to amplify the grandeur of the Western Paradise, represented by the *naijin*.

Right: An 1896 stone lithograph by Motoharu of the Founder's Hall at Higashi Honganji Temple.

Merging of Shinto and Buddhist Architecture

The introduction of Buddhism posed the problem of how to reconcile the new religion with indigenous Shinto beliefs and practices. The most ambitious solution was a doctrine that claimed that Shinto deities are incarnations or manifestations of Buddhas and Bodhisattvas. This merging of deities was sometimes accompanied by the merging of priestly functions and religious buildings as well.

Symbiotic Relationship

The mutual influence of Shinto and Buddhist architecture has already been noted. For example, many Shinto shrines adopted Buddhist structures, such as a two-story gate, a special hall for worshippers, connecting corridors, and vermilion colored wood. Many Buddhist temples, on the other hand, moved in the direction of a more indigenous kind of taste, characterized by asymmetry, the greater use of natural materials, and a sympathetic adaptation of buildings to the natural surroundings. Later developments, however, went beyond mutual influence to religious eclecticism – the merging of Shinto and Buddhist beliefs and practices.

This eclecticism took a variety of forms. A common practice in the early days of Buddhism in Japan was to placate local deities who might be disturbed at the intrusion of the newer religion into their territories, and to entice these local *kami* to provide protection for Buddhist temples. This was done by building Buddhist temples near Shinto shrines or constructing Shinto shrines on the grounds of Buddhist temples. In return, Buddhist priests offered help to *kami* who, like most other beings, were believed to be incapable of escaping the endless round of birth and rebirth by themselves. Help was provided by building Buddhist structures on Shinto compounds and by reading Buddhist scriptures in front of Shinto shrines.

Pairing Shinto and Buddhist Deities

One of the earliest proponents of religious syncretism in Japan was En-no-Gyōja (born in the seventh century) who purportedly was convinced that the *kami* of various mountains in Japan were really manifestations of the cosmic Buddha. The founder of Shingon, Kūkai, systematized this concept in the ninth century and developed the doctrine of Ryōbu Shinto, which means "Shinto of Double Aspects." In Shingon belief, the universe, though One, has two dimensions. The phenomenal dimension is the realm of anything that can be experienced by the five senses. Behind this dimension lies a noumenal realm, which can be experienced in a mystical fashion through appropriate ceremonies. Shingon theologians identified Shinto deities as concrete manifestations of Buddhist deities, which generally represent more abstract metaphysical qualities.

Above: Kannonji, a Tendai Buddhist temple in Shiga Prefecture. In front of the main door of the temple is a gong such as those used to announce one's presence to the resident *kami* of a Shinto shrine. The gong is rung by pulling on the rope. This is a good example of religious syncretism.

Right: Some of the buildings at Kyoto's Kitano Tenmangū Shinto Shrine in 1757, showing Buddhist buildings such as a Tahōtō style pagoda, Buddha Hall, Sutra Hall, and the main shrine complex. The shrine still exists, but the Buddhist structures have been removed. Drawing based on a model at the National Museum of Japanese History.

Layout of Kitano Tenmangū

1 Tenmangū Shrine
2 Buddha Hall
3 Sutra Hall
4 Tahōtō style Pagoda

Left: An 1896 stone lithograph by Motoharu of the Shinto gate in front of the entrance to Kitano Tenmangū Shrine, depicted in the drawing on page 76.

Combining Religious Functions

From the thirteenth through to the nineteenth century, it was not uncommon to combine both religions practically, as well as theoretically. For example, Shinto and Buddhist religious objects were mixed in the same building, and ceremonial activities were conducted by a single priest. In such cases, the two religions were almost indistinguishable. This religious syncretism was eventually accepted by most people and remained influential until the Meiji Restoration of 1868, when the two religions were separated and Shinto became the State religion, whose primary political function was to promote nationalism. Despite this forced separation, there are many shrines and temples that still show traces of religious syncretism today.

Hachiman Shrine

An interesting example of religious syncretism is Usa Hachiman Shrine in Kyushu. The god of war, Hachiman, who first manifested itself in 571, was believed by Ryōbu Shinto priests to be an incarnation of Amida Buddha. As a result, Usa Hachiman Shrine came to incorporate many Buddhist features, such as a belfry and Buddhist chapels. Today, a lotus pond near the entrance is one of the few remaining Buddhist traces.

Left: Yashima Shrine, on the grounds of Tōji Temple in Kyoto, exemplifies the incorporation of Shinto shrines into the grounds of Buddhist temples, a practice that is still common today.

The Way of the Warrior

Toward the end of the Heian Period, a series of wars between the Taira and Minamoto clans ultimately resulted in victory for the Minamoto. Determined to escape the influence of the effete culture of Kyoto, the Minamoto established a military shogunate in Kamaku ra and laid the basis for a feudal society governed by the principles of *bushidō*, the Way of the Warrior.

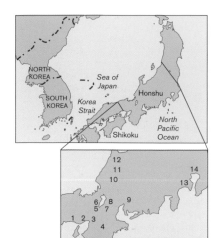

1 Himeiji Castle
2 Kakurinji Temple (Kakogawa City)
3 Osaka
4 Heijōkyō (Nara)
5 Hideyoshi's Fushimi Castle
6 Heiankyō (Kyoto)
7 Onjōji Temple (Ōtsu)
8 Nobunaga's Azuchi Castle
9 Inuyama
10 Ichijōdani
11 Eiheiji
12 Kanazawa
13 Kamakura
14 Edo

Kamakura Period (1185–1333)

Under the new military regime at Kamakura, founded by Minamoto Yoritomo, the samurai (*bushi*) became the ruling class. A hierarchical system was established in which samurai retainers owed fealty to their clan lords (*daimyo*), who, in turn, were under the control of the shogun, the supreme military ruler. The shogun received his appointment from the emperor, who retained symbolic power. This military system of government was known as the *bakufu*.

In contrast to an emphasis on delicate, refined beauty, characteristic of the Kyoto Court, the new samurai class emphasized simplicity, strength, and realism. Yoritomo rebuilt Tōdaiji and Kōfukuji temples in Nara, which had been burned during the clan wars at the end of the Heian Period. Rebuilding Tōdaiji took 20 years and involved a small army of carpenters and craftsmen. The resulting Great Buddha style had a heroic quality that symbolized the determination of the Kamakura shogunate to re-establish an effective central government.

The turmoil at the beginning of the Kamakura Period gave rise to new "Pure Land" Buddhist denominations such as Jōdo, which developed out of the Amida Buddhism of the preceding Heian Period. Japanese monks also went to China to study Zen Buddhism. They brought Zen back to Japan in the latter part of the Kamakura Period where it made a major contribution to samurai culture in the Muromachi Period which followed.

The Kamakura shogunate was sorely tested when the Mongols attempted twice to conquer Japan with the largest naval armada ever assembled. On both occasions, the Mongol navy was destroyed off the coast of Kyushu by typhoons, which were called *kamikaze* (divine winds). The cost of building military fortifications in Kyushu contributed to the downfall of the Minamoto clan. It was succeeded by the Ashikaga clan, which moved its military capital to the Muromachi area of Kyoto. As a result, Kyoto became the capital of both the imperial court and the military shogunate.

Muromachi (Ashikaga) Period (1333–1573)

Zen Buddhism appealed to the warrior class because of its emphasis upon intuitive awareness and aesthetic expression rather than upon esoteric beliefs and practices. Zen stimulated, or lent its support to numerous art forms such as *suiboku* (black ink) painting, calligraphy, flower arranging, the tea ceremony, landscape gardens, Noh drama, and the martial arts. Mastering an art form was perceived as a way to discipline the mind and body, thus resulting in practical benefits useful to a warrior.

Samurai Residences

There are no remains of samurai residences from the Kamakura Period. However, it is known from archaeological work that samurai houses were situated on flat land or on slightly sloping ground at the foot of a hill. Houses were usually surrounded by walls and moats. A moat was important not only for defense, but also for storing water for agricultural purposes in the surrounding area. This model of the house of a samurai who worked for the Kamakura government was constructed on the basis of picture scrolls from that era. The main building (Omoya) for the master and connected buildings were similar to the Shinden style. The main difference was that Shinden style buildings were normally roofed with cypress bark, whereas the house shown here uses a combination of thatch and boards. There were several subsidiary buildings for retainers, as well as a cooking shed, stables, a pit house for servants, and a vegetable garden.

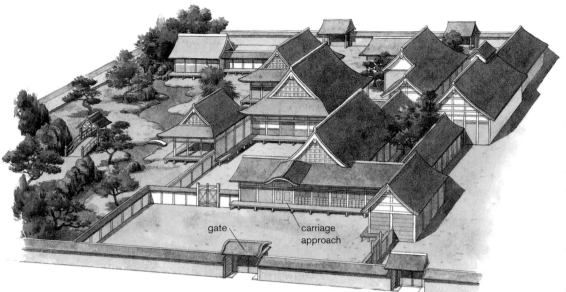

gate   carriage
        approach

Left: The Hosokawa Mansion as depicted in a sixteenth-century screen painting at the National Museum of Japanese History of street scenes in and around Kyoto. The Hosokawa family was the hereditary vassal of the Ashikaga shoguns. The Hosokawa Mansion represents an adaptation of Shinden style architecture, as was the custom among upper-class samurai of the period. The diagonal placement of the three main buildings is similar to that of the Shoin style developed later.

Zen Buddhism also influenced the architecture of the period. It introduced new principles of temple construction from China and had an impact upon the development of samurai houses. Its crowning architectural achievement, however, was the creation of the teahouse, in which simplicity, naturalness, and understatement, expressed in terms such as *wabi* and *sabi*, emphasized the beauty of the tea ceremony.

Other examples of Muromachi architecture are the famous temple villas, Kinkakuji (Temple of the Golden Pavilion) and Ginkakuji (Temple of the Silver Pavilion), in Kyoto. Eventually, the Ashikaga shogunate lost its control over the other clans and more than a decade of warfare (the Ōnin War) ensued, resulting in great destruction and the impoverishment of the imperial court in Kyoto.

Momoyama Period (1573–1600)

Japan was reunified by a succession of three great military leaders. In 1573, Oda Nobunaga defeated the Ashikaga shogunate to take control of central Japan. He constructed Japan's first important castle, Azuchijō, on the banks of Lake Biwa, near Kyoto. Its colorful exterior was matched only by the opulence of the interior. Azuchijō was destroyed by fire in 1582, the year in which Nobunaga was assassinated. Despite the brevity of its existence, Nobunaga's castle had a strong influence on subsequent castles.

After Nobunaga's death, Toyotomi Hideyoshi assumed power and continued the process of military unification. Possibly because of his humble peasant background, Hideyoshi was extravagant in the demonstration of his wealth, constructing lavish palaces and castles, such as Fushimi Castle, south of Kyoto, which burned in 1600. Hideyoshi also reconstructed Osaka Castle, one of the major fortresses of its day. After his death in 1598, his son was defeated in 1600 by Tokugawa Ieyasu, and the military capital was moved to Edo (present-day Tokyo). The move marked the beginning of the Edo (or Tokugawa) Period, characterized by 250 years of relative peace and stability, as well as isolation from the West and its influences.

Left: Model of Nobunaga's Azuchi Castle based upon floor plans derived from various documents of the period by Naitō Masa. The model upon which this drawing is based is the property of Azuchi Town Office, Shiga Prefecture.

New Principles in Residential Architecture

Right: The study of Yoshimasa, the eighth Ashikaga shogun, is located in the Tōgudō of Ginkakuji in Kyoto. It has a built-in desk and shelves at one end, and is the oldest extant Shoin style room in Japan. The built-in desk has sliding paper doors (*shōji*) behind it. The study is known as Dōjinsai.

Below: The Kachōden room in Shōrenin, a Tendai temple in Kyoto, is a typical Shoin style room. The *tokonoma* is between the staggered shelves on the left and the built-in desk on the further wall. The room is divided from the adjacent area by an elaborately carved transom (*ramma*).

Early modern residential architecture has its roots in the Shoin style of the Muromachi Period, which gradually developed out of the Shinden style of Heian Period mansions. Shoin rooms, used as studies in the living quarters of monasteries, or for entertaining guests in the villas of shoguns, include features such as a recessed alcove (*tokonoma*), built-in desk, staggered shelves, and decorative doors.

Priest Residences

Living quarters of priests are just as important as the residences of aristocrats and samurai for understanding the development of residential architecture in Japan. During the Asuka and Nara Periods, the living quarters for Buddhist priests normally were built in a symmetrical U shape, immediately to the back of one of the main temple buildings. During the Heian Period, Buddhist continental architecture was influenced by Japanese taste, with its preference for asymmetry and a less formal layout. As a result, priests started to build their living quarters in more private regions of the temple grounds. Since most priests were from aristocratic families, they adopted the Shinden style of architecture used in aristocratic villas.

The late Heian and Kamakura Periods saw the introduction of new types of Buddhism that solicited their priests from the ranks of commoners rather than noble families. As a result, many priests were not able to afford Shinden style buildings and lived in simpler Shoin style structures. Literally, *shoin*

means "writing hall" or "study," which accounts for features such as a built-in desk and bookshelves.

Many of the Ashikaga shoguns in the Muromachi Period became priests after they left the post of shogun. Their retirement villas, such as Kinkakuji and Ginkakuji, adopted the general concept of a monastic living area, including one or more Buddha halls and several Shinden style residential buildings. These buildings often incorporated a Shoin style room, which was used as a study or for entertaining guests.

Architectural Features

In addition to the four basic features of the Shoin style (recessed alcove, shelves, desk, and decorative doors), not necessarily all found in the same room, a Shoin style room included wall-to-wall *tatami* mats, beveled square posts, coved and/or coffered ceilings, *fusuma* (sliding screens used to divide interior space), *shōji* (wooden-lattice exterior sliding doors covered with translucent rice paper), and *amado* (heavy wooden doors that could be closed at night or during inclement weather).

Later, more formal Shoin style rooms were developed for entertaining important guests. A raised floor at the end of the room, containing the *tokonoma* and staggered shelves, was where the host and his guests sat. Formal Shoin style rooms were commonly used by the abbots of monasteries or by shoguns. In the Edo Period, the Shoin style gave rise to the Sukiya style, in which numerous variations were added to suit the taste of the owner.

Left: Ōhiroma (Audience Hall), the most important building in Ninomaru Palace, on the grounds of Nijō Castle in Kyoto, has a large *tokonoma* at the end, with staggered shelves and decorative doors to the right. To the left of the *tokonoma* is a built-in desk. The raised floor is where the shogun sat with his guests when he visited from Edo.

Below left: Seisonkaku Villa in Kanazawa, a two-story building with a hipped roof, was built by Maeda Nariyasu, the thirteenth Kaga *daimyo*, for his mother as a retirement residence. The Ekken-no-ma (guest chamber) on the first floor has all of the features of a formal Shoin style room: *tokonoma*, built-in desk, staggered shelves, and decorative doors. It also has a raised floor and an elaborate transom. Photograph courtesy of Seisonkaku.

Oldest Existing Shoin Style Buildings

The only extant example of Shoin style architecture from the Muromachi Period is the Tōgudō at Ginkakuji Temple. Daigoji Temple in Kyoto has a building constructed in 1598 that looks like a Shinden style structure from the outside but has a Shoin style interior.

Well-known Shoin style buildings from the early Edo Period are the guest halls of two sub-temples of the Tendai monastery Onjōji, in the city of Ōtsu, Shiga Prefecture. One of these has all four basic features of the Shoin style: recessed alcove, staggered shelves, built-in desk, and decorative doors. Most Shoin style rooms possess only two or three of these features.

Other important Edo Period examples are two Shoin style rooms at Nishi Honganji Temple in Kyoto, as well as two rooms in the Ninomaru Palace, built on the grounds of Nijō Castle, also in Kyoto, by Iemitsu, the third Tokugawa shogun, for the visit of the emperor in 1626.

Persistence and Spread of the Shoin Style

Shoin style architecture eventually was adopted by people of wealth and power from all walks of life. In addition to being used in palaces and important temples, Shoin style rooms or buildings were incorporated into the villas of high-ranking samurai families, and even the homes of wealthy farmers. The Shoin style reached its peak in the early part of the Edo Period. Shoin style rooms and buildings are still built today, primarily by temples attempting to regain past glory.

The primary reason for the persistence and spread of the Shoin style is that it reached a level of perfection in terms of tasteful elegance that has never been surpassed in Japanese architecture. The Shoin style is particularly important because of its influence on early modern residential architecture, which includes features such as *tatami* mats, flexible interiors divided by sliding paper doors (*fusuma*), recessed alcoves for art objects (*tokonoma*), and exterior sliding doors covered with translucent rice paper (*shōji*).

Below: The present *shinden* (main building) of Ninnaji Temple in Kyoto, established in 888 by the Emperor Uda, was rebuilt in 1911 using a mixture of Shinden and Shoin styles. The Ichi-no-ma room in the *shinden* is a formal Shoin style room where the abbot sits for audience.

Left: The grand reception room (Kairaku-no-ma) at Zanyūsō in Aichi Prefecture, built in 1917 by Tamasatu Teiichi, the second generation head of a wealthy family and a renowned votary of the tea ceremony, contains all the features of the formal Shoin style, including a deep recessed *tokonoma* alcove and accompanying *shōji* window, a hanging scroll, a built-in desk and staggered shelves, decorative doors, and wall-to-wall *tatami* mats. All the elements combine to achieve an unobstructed space and an atmosphere of calm and modest elegance.

Kinkakuji and Ginkakuji Temples

Above: An 1896 stone lithograph by Motoharu of Kinkakuji Temple.

Opposite: The Golden Pavilion at Kinkakuji is an eclectic combination of three different styles of architecture: Shinden, samurai, and Zen. The abundant use of gold leaf is balanced by the delicate curve of the eaves and the use of bark on the roof to create a graceful edifice that combines indigenous and Chinese influences in a surprisingly successful way.

Pages 86–7: Located on the northeastern edge of Kyōkochi Pond, the Golden Pavilion is positioned to afford a good view of the pond as well as the mountains to the west and north of Kyoto.

The Muromachi Period (1333–1573) was the Golden Age of Zen-inspired culture. Two of the best examples of Muromachi architecture are Kinkakuji (Temple of the Golden Pavilion) and Ginkakuji (Temple of the Silver Pavilion) in Kyoto. Constructed by the third and eighth Ashikaga shoguns for use as private residences, both compounds were converted to Zen temples after the deaths of their owners.

Kinkakuji (Temple of the Golden Pavilion)

There are no records of what the residences of shoguns looked like during the Kamakura Period. Since the samurai did not yet have their own distinct culture or architectural style, it is probable that the early shoguns borrowed the Shinden style from aristocrats. In the following Ashikaga Period, shogunal mansions continued to be built in the Shinden style, with a main building connected to several subsidiary buildings by covered corridors.

In 1397, the third Ashikaga shogun, Yoshimitsu, who had abdicated to his son so he could concentrate on religion and the arts, began constructing Kitayamaden (meaning North Mountain Villa), on the grounds of a dilapidated mansion of an old aristocratic family in Kyoto. The new villa consisted of several Shinden style buildings and a pavilion

covered with gold leaf, from whence derives the name Kinkaku (Golden Pavilion). According to records, Yoshimitsu and his wife used a Shinden style palace on the north of the compound as their private residence. A palace on the south was used for entertaining guests. By this time, the need had arisen for a more informal meeting and entertainment space, giving rise to a new style of building, the *kaisho*, which was added to the Shinden style buildings and the Golden Pavilion. Official meetings were held in one of the Shinden style buildings, after which the participants moved to the *kaisho*, where the shogun's art collections were displayed, for a more relaxed atmosphere.

Buildings were arranged around a boating and strolling garden, in the center of which was a lake that reflected the Golden Pavilion. This setting is called a "borrowed scenery" garden since it incorporates a view of a hill and gently sloping mountains to the west and north of Kyoto. When the villa was completed in 1408, Yoshimitsu held a grand party that lasted several days, which was attended by the emperor and his entourage.

After Yoshimitsu's death, the villa was turned into a Rinzai Zen temple, Rokuonji. Most of the original buildings were lost

Layout of Kinkakuji

1 Kinkaku (Golden Pavilion)
2 Hōjō
3 Kuri
4 Sekkatei Teahouse

in successive wars, until only the Kinkaku remained. Today, Rokuonji goes by the popular name of Kinkakuji, Temple of the Golden Pavilion. The famous pavilion was burned by a crazed priest in 1950, but a faithful replica was constructed in 1955. In 1987, a layer of gold leaf, five times the original thickness, was applied to the pavilion and the pictures on the ceilings were restored. The temple was designated a World Cultural Heritage Site in 1994.

Architecture of Kinkakuji

Kinkaku is a three-story pavilion about 12.5 meters high. It consists of three types of architecture skillfully blended in one building. The first floor, constructed of unpainted wood and white plaster, is in the Shinden palace style, consisting of a large open space surrounded by peripheral verandas under the eaves. Walls are composed primarily of two-part hinged shutters. The bottom halves can be removed, and the top halves can be raised and hooked to the soffit above to let in light and air.

The second floor, said to be in the samurai style, is a Buddha Hall with sliding wooden doors and removable latticed windows. It enshrines Kannon, goddess of mercy. The third floor is in the Zen style, with bell-shaped windows and paneled doors. Reflecting the religious eclecticism of Yoshimitsu, it enshrines a Jōdo style Amida Buddha and 25 Bodhisattvas. The inside and outside of both the second and third floors are covered with gold leaf – from whence the pavilion's popular name came. The pyramidal roof is thatched with shingles and topped with a gilt phoenix.

Below: The recently reconstructed Kuri at Kinkakuji is typical of the living quarters built for priests in most Zen monasteries. The sloping gabled roof, which is tiled, contains a *kemuri-dashi* (smoke vent) for the kitchen.

Ginkakuji (Temple of the Silver Pavilion)

Yoshimasa, the eighth Ashikaga shogun, tried to relive the golden years of his grandfather Yoshimitsu, who built Kinkakuji. Yoshimasa spent eight years constructing Higashiyamaden (meaning Eastern Mountain Villa), which originally contained 12 structures, including the Kannon Hall (popularly known as Ginkaku, the Silver Pavilion), the Tōgudō, a meditation room, and an informal building for entertaining guests (kaisho). Construction stopped with the death of Yoshimasa in 1490, before the Kannon Hall, the main building, was finished. As a result, the building was not covered with silver leaf, as originally planned. Higashiyamaden was the birthplace of so-called Higashiyama Culture since Yoshimasa's fondness for the arts stimulated the development of flower arranging, the tea ceremony, kōdō (the Way of Incense), and other art forms that thrive even today.

As in the case of Kinkakuji, after the death of Yoshimasa the villa was turned into a Zen temple, which became known as Jishōji. During the Edo Period, Jishōji came to be called Ginkakuji, Temple of the Silver Pavilion. Over time, most of the buildings were destroyed or allowed to deteriorate until eventually only the Kannon Hall and the Tōgudō remained. A Main Hall was added in the mid-Edo Period and a new Shoin style building was constructed in 1993.

Above: The Kannon Hall (Silver Pavilion) at Ginkakuji is a two-story structure inspired by the Temple of the Golden Pavilion. Similarities can be seen in the general proportions, line of the eaves, use of bark shingles on the roofs, rectangular openings on the first floor, cusped windows (katō-mado) on the top floors, and graceful verandas with railings. Though the building was never covered with silver leaf as originally intended, it has its own charm. Many Japanese prefer it to Kinkakuji because of the modest way in which it blends into the surroundings. It is a fitting symbol of the aesthetic values of wabi and sabi, developed in the tea ceremony, of which the eighth shogun was so fond.

Layout of Ginkakuji

1 Ginkaku (Kannon Hall or Silver Pavilion)
2 Kōgetsudai (Gravel Cone or "Moon-viewing Dais")
3 Ginsadan (Sea of Silver Sand)
4 Tōgudō

Architecture of Ginkakuji

The Kannon Hall is a two-story edifice consisting of a Shoin style first floor, where Yoshimasa practiced Zen meditation, and an upper-floor worship hall with paneled walls. The upper floor has cusped windows with paper sliding doors. It houses a gilt image of Kannon, the goddess of mercy.

The Tōgudō, built in 1485, has a wood-floored altar room that originally housed an image of Amida Buddha, and three rooms with *tatami* mats. One of the latter, consisting of 4.5 mats, is the oldest extant Shoin style room in Japan. It is considered to be a proto-type of the Sōan style ("grass hut") tearoom, described later. Small rooms such as these *tatami* rooms were something new, as the standard room size in Shinden style buildings of upper-class aristocrats was much larger. Reflecting the eclecticism of Yoshimasa, the Tōgudō, with its Amida Buddha, faces an early example of a Zen style stroll garden, constructed around a pond.

Above: A striking feature of the garden at Ginkakuji is a raked gravel area with a perfectly shaped gravel cone called Kōgetsudai, or "moon-viewing dais."

Left: The Tōgudō at Ginkakuji is a single-story building with a hipped-and-gable roof covered with Japanese cypress bark. The Silver Pavilion and Tōgudō, much more restrained than the pavilion at Kinkakuji, have been designated as National Treasures.

The Way of Tea

Opposite: The teahouse at the old reconstructed Zanyūsō is entered via a 2 foot (60 cm) high "crawl door," originally designed to make samurai leave their swords (and egos) behind and to come in with a pure and humble mind. Inside, all participants of the tea ceremony are considerd equal. The soft outline of the bamboo and reed lattice is visible through the *shōji* screens. The lower parts of the mud plaster walls are covered with Japanese *washi* paper to protect the guests' clothing.

The tea ceremony had humble beginnings. Tea was originally employed by Buddhist monks to keep them awake during meditation. Later, tea was adopted by aristocrats for use in elaborate tea tasting games. Beginning in the Kamakura Period, tea drinking developed into a sophisticated ritual with different schools. The architecture associated with the Way of Tea (*chanoyu* or *sadō*) continues to make its influence felt.

Development of the Tea Ceremony

A tea ceremony can be conducted in a special room included in a building such as a private dwelling, palace, temple, or castle; or the ceremony can be conducted in a building con-

Jo-an Teahouse

Jo-an Teahouse in Uraku Garden, Inuyama City, is a National Treasure constructed in 1618 by Oda Uraku, a disciple of Sen-no-Rikyū. It is built in the Sōan "grass hut" style. Though the teahouse is very small in size, Uraku's genius can be seen in features such as window openings covered with vertical bamboo slats that admit light and air, the lower portion of a wall covered with old calendars, and a natural pole at the corner of the hearth. Other interesting features are a crawl door, a triangular wall adjacent to the *tokonoma* (not shown in the drawing below), a black lacquered wood area near the hearth, and an interior arched doorway.

structed especially for that purpose. Here, the term "teahouse" is used to refer to both types.

In the Kamakura Period, tea drinking was endorsed by Zen Buddhism, which was newly introduced from China. Zen exerted a good deal of influence upon the development of the Way of Tea in the Muromachi and Momoyama Periods. The individual who made the greatest impact upon this transformation into a refined aesthetic ceremony with profound philosophical and religious connotations was Sen-no-Rikyū (1521–91), the personal tea master of the military ruler Nobunaga, as well as his successor, Hideyoshi.

Sen-no-Rikyū favored austerity, with an emphasis upon the aesthetic concepts of *sabi* (the patina that comes with age) and *wabi* (things that are simple, natural, and imperfect). These qualities are manifested in the tranquil garden setting, the austerity of the teahouse and its use of natural materials, the unassuming tea ceremony vessels, and the seemingly effortless and graceful movements of the tea master. It is said that Rikyū's teahouses became smaller as Hideyoshi's Osaka Castle grew larger – an implied criticism of the often extravagant taste of the great warlord. Eventually, the two had an unfortunate parting of the ways.

Later History of the Tea Ceremony

The tea ceremony was passed on to three of Sen-no-Rikyū's relatives, including his stepson, each of whom started a different tea lineage. All three lineages continued to favor Rikyū's emphasis upon austerity and understatement and to employ the Sōan (grass hut) style teahouse, which is small and simple. Rikyū also had seven other disciples, mainly Hideyoshi's samurai retainers, who adopted Shoin style architecture for their teahouses. Shoin teahouses, befitting their aristocratic origins, were larger and less rustic than their Sōan cousins. By the beginning of the Edo Period, there was a tendency for both styles to adopt specific features from each other.

Common Features of Teahouses

There is disagreement about the original inspiration for Sōan teahouse architecture, but most historians agree that one influence was Shoin style architecture. Another was the Japanese farmhouse, with its use of natural materials and relaxed, rustic atmosphere. Farmhouse features were, of course, reworked to achieve the subtle religious and aesthetic meanings appropriate to the tea ceremony.

A teahouse is composed of two main elements: the building itself and the garden. Access to the building is sometimes through a low "crawl door," originally designed to prevent samurai from entering with their swords. It also symbolizes the fact that once inside, all participants are equal, regardless of rank. The interior consists of *tatami* mats where the participants sit, a recessed alcove

(*tokonoma*) for a hanging scroll and flower arrangement, and one or more optional anterooms where preparations are done. The size of the room ranges from two to eight or more *tatami* mats, depending upon the type of ceremony. Before Sen-no-Rikyū's time, walls were made of mud covered with white paper. After Rikyū, plain mud walls became popular, sometimes painted the color of green tea powder or given a red cast from mixing red shells or husks with the mud. The lower portion of these mud walls had to be faced with Japanese paper or boards to keep clothing from getting soiled. Windows consist of holes of different sizes and shapes, covered with materials such as bamboo slats or Japanese rice paper. Natural poles used in the interior are debarked and often painted with a red pigment mixed with soot to create a subdued, dark color that complements the beauty of the tea utensils.

The teahouse garden is an integral part of the setting. It is usually divided into two areas by gates. The outer area provides covered seating where guests wait quietly to be summoned by the tea master to the ceremony, as well as an ornamental privy. The inner area may have additional seating, a water basin for washing hands, and stepping stones on which guests are expected to walk. Larger stones indicate where one may pause before continuing the approach to the teahouse. The inner area also may contain a stone lantern and some trees or shrubs.

Teahouse Gardens

The garden is an integral part of a teahouse. Its purpose is to prepare one for participation in a tea ceremony by providing a serene natural setting. After entering the gate to the garden, participants sit in a covered waiting area for the tea ceremony to begin. At the invitation of the tea master, participants wash their hands and mouth from water in a rock basin and proceed to the teahouse on stepping stones, pausing on the larger stones for a brief moment of reflection. They leave their foot apparel at the entrance, before stooping to pass through the small "crawl door." These features are illustrated by these photographs taken at Urakuen in Inuyama, Aichi Prefecture, in which Jo-an (a small Sōan style teahouse) and Shōdenin (a large Shoin style building), as well as several other buildings, are located, having been moved there in 1970.

Right: Layout of the garden area surrounding the Jo-an, Shōdenin, and Gen-an buildings in Uraku Garden.

The stone walkway leading to Jo-an Teahouse.

The Kayamon Gate is constructed of poles covered with a grass roof. On top of the roof is a bamboo and log frame designed to help hold the grass in place.

Shōdenin Shoin

Gen-en Teahouse

Jo-an Teahouse

The entrance area to the Gen-an, where shoes are left before entering the teahouse through the small crawl door. Above and to the left of the door is a rack where, in the old days, samurai would leave their swords. Above the door is an opening covered with a bamboo lattice that can be adjusted by a sliding window constructed of a wood frame covered with rice paper.

A rock basin (*tsukubai*) fed by water running through a bamboo tube.

The waiting place (*machiai*) consists of a bench in a simple enclosure with mud walls, covered on the inside with rice paper to protect one's clothing.

Feudal Period Temples

Above: Detail of the Nandaimon Gate at Tōdaiji, showing the multi-tiered bracketing system.

Below: Nandaimon Gate at Tōdaiji. After being burned in 1180, it was rebuilt in 1181 by Chōgen who studied Daibutsuyō style architecture in China.

Buddhist temples in the Nara Period, based on Korean and Chinese prototypes, were relatively consistent in style. This was not the case thereafter. In the Heian Period, Amida Buddhism gave rise to new denominations and architectural styles. In the Kamakura Period, the Great Buddha and Zen styles were introduced from Song China. Eclectic styles incorporated elements from both, as well as from earlier periods.

Wayō Style

The original building techniques brought from Korea and China were altered to suit a different environment in Japan. One of the primary improvements was to strengthen joints, making the building more resistant to earthquakes and typhoons. Early improvements, as well as design innovations, such as the double roof system, constitute the Wayō (Japanese) style.

Great Buddha Style

The Daibutsuyō (Great Buddha style) was used by priest Chōgen, who studied Song Dynasty building techniques in China, in the rebuilding of Tōdaiji Temple, beginning in 1181, after the Nara Period temple burned the previous year. The Great South Gate (Nandaimon) at Tōdaiji remains from Chōgen's time. The main feature of the new technique was the use of several layers of brackets to support a massive roof. The brackets were sunk into the columns and reinforced by lateral ties that pierced the center of the posts and extended the entire length of

the building. Though this technique was efficient and provided a feeling of simplicity, it involved making holes in the pillars. This technique weakened the structure and was not much used in later periods. The Tōdaiji complex was reconstructed in the Kamakura Period and again around 1700, after disastrous fires. The present Daibutsuden (Great Hall), though only two-thirds of its original size, is still the largest wooden building under one roof in the world.

Zen Style

The Zenshūyō, or Karayō (Chinese style), was developed in Song China and introduced to Japan in the Kamakura Period by two priests who had studied Zen in China: Myōan Eisai (1141–1215) and Eihei Dōgen (1200–53). Very few original Zen buildings remain from the Kamakura Period. Reconstructed buildings, however, are generally quite faithful to the original.

Distinguishing features of the Zen style are as follows. Pillars, beveled at both the top and bottom, sit on carved stone blocks (*soban*), resting on base stones that are placed on a raised platform faced with stone. The square pillars and beams, usually painted vermilion, are slender compared to the posts of previous styles. Eaves brackets rest not only on posts, as in the Wayō and Great Buddha styles, but on the inter-columnar spaces as well. Doors and windows are frequently cusped. Most Zen style buildings have a hipped-and-gable roof (*irimoya*), with a pent roof (*mokoshi*) below, giving the appearance of a two-story building. Originally, roofs were tiled in the Chinese style. Later, tile often was replaced with wood shingles or thatch.

The plan of a Zen monastery as a whole is symmetrical, with the main buildings arranged on a central axis. Zen buildings were originally connected by covered corridors to create several courtyards – an arrangement that still can be seen at Eiheiji Temple, one of the headquarters of Sōtō Zen.

Eclectic Style

Toward the end of the Kamakura Period, the different styles began adopting specific features from each other to create what is called the Secchūyō or eclectic style. This created a great variety of styles that are difficult to categorize, and resulted in a reduction in the number of temples built in the pure "Japanese" style. A good example of the eclectic style is the

1 Sanmon (Main Gate)
2 Chūjakumon Gate
3 Butsuden (Buddha Hall)
4 Hattō (Dharma Hall)
5 Sōdō (Priests' Hall)
6 Tosu (Toilet)
7 Sanshōkaku (Reception Hall)
8 Shidoden (Memorial Hall)
9 Shōrō (Bell Tower)
10 Chokushimon (Imperial Gate)
11 Daikuin (Kitchen)

The eaves brackets of the Buddha Hall at Eiheiji are so closely spaced that they create a baroque effect.

Eiheiji

Layout of some of the most important buildings at Eiheiji, one of the two headquarters of Sōtō Zen Buddhism, located in Fukui Prefecture. The main buildings, on a central axis, are attached to buildings on either side by covered corridors to create multiple courtyards that extend up the slope of the hill to the Dharma Hall on top. The compound is surrounded by forest and incorporates enormous cryptomeria trees planted by the founder and his successors hundreds of years ago. Based on a painting at Eiheiji.

Covered corridors, with long flights of steps, connect many of the 70 or so buildings at Eiheiji Monastery.

Sanmon Gate at Tōfukuji Temple in Kyoto. One of the Five Great Zen temples of Kyoto, Tōfukuji was completed in 1255 but burned three times in the fourteenth century. The Sanmon, the oldest surviving Zen main gate in Japan, was reconstructed in 1405, combining the Zen and Great Buddha styles.

Perhaps the most famous example of the eclectic style is the Main Hall of Kakurinji Temple in Kakogawa City, Hyogo Prefecture. Built in 1397, the building is basically constructed in the Wayō style, with details from the Great Buddha and Zen styles added.

Left: The Sanmon Gate at Tōfukuji Temple in Kyoto is a good example of the eclectic style. The posts are rounded, as in the Great Buddha style, in contrast to the squared, more slender posts of the pure Zen style. On the other hand, the Sanmon has a Zen style support system for the eaves: brackets rest on posts and brackets between the posts rest on horizontal beams. This contrasts with the pure Great Buddha style in which brackets are lined up with the posts.

The Ichijōdani Historical Site

Top: Partially excavated site of the Asakura mansion, with the entrance gate in the distance.

Above: Bridge across the moat surrounding the Asakura mansion site. The mansion was surrounded by an earthen wall with a tiled roof. The gate is from the early Edo Period.

Below: Reconstruction of part of the Asakura mansion, based on a model at the Ichijōdani Asakura-shi Iseki Shiryōkan (Ichijōdani Asakura Historic Site Museum). The mansion included 17 buildings, mostly constructed in the Shinden style, with raised floors, verandas, board or bark roofs, and connecting corridors.

A good deal is known about Momoyama castles, but little is known about the medieval towns that grew up around them. Ichijōdani Historical Site in Fukui Prefecture is unique in that it contains the remains of a grand castle town with a graceful culture that was burned in 1573 after the Asakura *daimyo* lost a battle against Oda Nobunaga, who was in the process of unifying the country.

Designation as a Historic Site

When Ichijōdani was burned, the remains of the town were covered with ashes and, subsequently, with dirt. Its existence was known for a long time, and in 1930 the Japanese government designated it as a Special Historic Site and Place of Scenic Beauty. An effort has been made since 1967 to excavate and research the area, and to uncover the shape of the whole town. In 1971, the Japanese government enlarged the protected area to 278 hectares and established it as a historic park. In 1992, four Asakura gardens were named Special Places of Scenic Beauty. The objective of the reconstruction is to preserve the numerous excavated artifacts in a re-created town that provides a suitable context that is easy for the general public to observe and understand.

History

During the latter part of the Muromachi Period (1333–1573) and continuing into the Momoyama Period (1573–1600), there was a movement among farmers, merchants, and warriors to organize in order to prtect their interests. *Daimyo* (local clan lords), such as the Asakura family, were also constructing strong fortresses from which they could expand their territories and establish a secure organization of samurai retainers under their control. The first Asakura *daimyo* ruled the Ichijōdani area around 1450. The fifth Asakura *daimyo* was defeated by Oda Nobunaga, who promptly set fire to the entire area. Shibata Katsuie, who became *daimyo* after Asakura's defeat, built his castle in nearby Kitanoshō (present-day Fukui City). As a result, the Ichijōdani site was left undisturbed for many years.

Setting

Ichijōdani is situated in a narrow valley with mountains on both sides. At two points where the valley was narrow, earth mounds and moats were constructed to control entry and exit to a 1.7 kilometer long area where the town was built. Recent archeological research has revealed that the Asakura family built the town according to a master plan. The feudal class system was not yet well defined and some of the samurai were also engaged in farming or business. The Asakura ordered their important retainers to live at Ichijōdani, partly to reinforce its security, and partly to remove the warriors from their own territories, where they were busy building their own power bases. In addition, Asakura sent his own representatives to the domains of his samurai to oversee their operations and to increase Asakura influence. At its height, Ichijōdani was a bustling town with around 10,000 residents.

Roads, ranging in width from two to eight meters, were built through the area and blocks were set aside for the 40 or so temples, as well as housing for warriors, merchants, and craftsmen. Large samurai residences were surrounded by an earthen wall with a gate opening onto the road. In contrast, the modest houses of commoners face directly onto the road.

The Asakura Mansion

The Asakuras lived in a housing complex next to the Ichijōdani River at the foot of Mount Ichijō, upon which stood their castle. The Asakura's mansion was surrounded by a moat and earth walls with corner turrets, except for the side backing onto the hill with its castle. Inside the walled compound were 17 buildings. The first building after entering the front gate was where the retainers stayed, and next to it was the main building complex, containing the *shuden* in which formal audiences were held, living quarters for the family, and guest rooms. Stables and auxiliary buildings were along the north wall. The compound also had a garden with rock formations and a spring-fed pond.

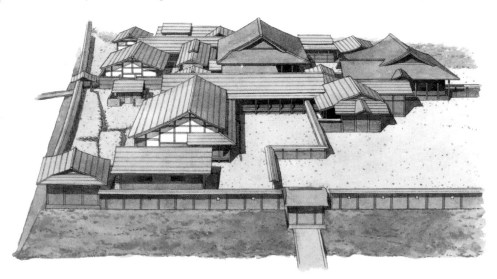

Reconstructing Historical Sites

Accuracy, based on available facts, is the most important requirement for reconstructing non-extant buildings. Nevertheless, some amount of inference is necessary.

Archaeological Evidence

In some cases, historians have been able to determine the size and shape of buildings at the Ichijōdani site from archaeological evidence, such as the placement of foundation stones and markings left on the stones by posts. Pieces of original construction materials, such as lumber, plaster, and metal, have been found, as well as ornaments, tools, and numerous artifacts. Sometimes the absence of certain materials is significant. For example, it has been determined that tile roofs were not used at Ichijōdani since no tiles have been found.

Other Types of Evidence

More detailed information had to be inferred on the basis of buildings still remaining from that period. This included aristocratic structures such as Tōgudō Hall at Ginkakuji Temple in Kyoto (1485) and the living quarters of the head priest at Daisenin, a sub-temple of Daitokuji Zen monastery in Kyoto (1513), as well as the homes of average people, such as the Hakogi family house in Hyogo Prefecture (late Muromachi Period) and the Furui family house in Hyōgo Prefecture (also late Muromachi Period). A number of Rakuchū-Rakugai-zu folding screens from the Momoyama Period, depicting street scenes in and around Kyoto, also provided useful information. These reference materials provided clues to variables such as the size and arrangement of posts and beams, as well as how these were fastened together.

Preliminary building blueprints were presented to the reconstruction committee, composed of experts provided by the Fukui prefectural government and the national government. After lengthy debate and careful examination, a final plan was prepared using computer graphics. Next, the committee located carpenters with experience in restoring old buildings, conducted field trips to observe old buildings from that period, and gathered building materials and tools used in the Muromachi Period. Finally, carpenters reconstructed a number of buildings using old tools and construction methods whenever possible.

Typical metal ornaments and handles used on doors.

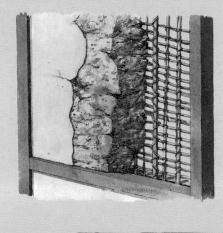

Constructing the wall of a building. After the posts and beams are in place, the space between the posts is filled with strips of wood and bamboo fastened together to form a lattice. This lattice is then covered on both sides with mud mixed with straw, which is then covered with cloth and plastered.

Remnant of a wood sill with channels for sliding doors.

Excavations

The Asakuras had their own resident craftsmen who produced a variety of items such as coins, prayer beads, and guns. Excavations have uncovered more than 1,500,000 items of pottery and other implements, including imports from China and other parts of Japan. Over 3,000 stone Buddhist statues and pagodas have been excavated and preserved and displayed in their natural settings.

Reconstruction of the Buildings

In order to preserve the numerous archaeological artifacts and to make it easier for the general public to understand the research findings, reconstruction of several buildings in Ichijōdani has been carried out, including *buke yashiki* (samurai houses) and *machiya* (town houses) along a 200-meter stretch of road running north and south, across the Ichijōdani River from the Asakura residence. Reconstruction was carried out in accordance with computer graphics based upon the archaeological evidence.

The size of a samurai residence depended upon his rank. Regardless of size, samurai compounds were enclosed by earthen walls with gates that opened onto the street. The spacious courtyards contained a variety of subsidiary buildings, including a toilet, well, storehouses, and workshops for artisans.

In contrast, the small dwellings of the commoners (*machiya*) were simple buildings around six meters wide and 12 to 15 meters deep, surrounded by a brushwood fence. Some commoner dwellings were constructed in the *hirairi* style (with the entrance on the long side, parallel to the roof ridge), and some in the *tsumairi* style (with the entrance on the gable end). Most *machiya* faced onto the road.

Above: Canopies above the slatted windows on these reconstructed *machiya* protect the doors on the gable ends (*tsumairi* style). Board roofs are weighted down with rocks. Interiors comprise a dirt floor and a raised area covered with boards.

Castles and Castle Culture

Above: Hirosaki Castle in Aomori Prefecture, rebuilt in 1810, is one of the smallest castles in Japan.

Opposite: Built in 1603, the three-story Hikone Castle is small but one of the most beautiful in Japan.

Below: Matsumoto Castle in Nagano Prefecture, built in 1596, is one of the twelve remaining orginal castles in Japan.

Constant warfare during the chaotic years of decentralized feudalism led to the spread of castle culture, which reached its height in the Momoyama Period (1573–1600). In the following Edo Period (1600–1868), castles were strictly regulated, and during the Meiji Period (1868–1912), many were destroyed. More were lost to neglect and World War II. Today, only 12 original castles survive.

Castles in the Azuchi-Momoyama Period

Although no longer in existence, Nobunaga's castle at Azuchi and Hideyoshi's castle at Momoyama have given their names to the period in which Japan was unified by a succession of three military leaders: Oda Nobunaga, Toyotomi Hideyoshi, and Tokugawa Ieyasu. The designation of this period as Azuchi-Momoyama (usually abbreviated to Momoyama) is appropriate in light of the significance of castles as the centers of a distinctive new type of urban culture associated with the growth of castle towns. Although a few castles, such as Marugame, Bicchū-Matsuyama, Kochi, Hirosaki, and Matsuyama were constructed in the Edo Period, in general castle culture reached its peak in the Momoyama Period, after which it gradually declined as a result of unification.

Types of Castles

There are four basic types of castles. Mountaintop castles (*yamashiro*) were constructed on the tops of mountains where they were protected by the rough terrain as well as the reluctance of Japanese to attack the habitat of spirits associated with nature. Because they were used only in time of war, mountaintop castles were small, semi-permanent structures that lacked the type of fortifications found in many other castles. An example of an original mountaintop castle is Maruoka Castle in Fukui, constructed in 1576. A few mountaintop castles, such as Kururi Castle in Chiba Prefecture, have been rebuilt, most commonly with modern fire-resistant materials such as concrete blocks.

Flatland–mountain castles (*hirayamajiro*), built on a hill or high plateau in the middle of a lord's domain, included residences for the lord and his chief retainers. Because they lacked the natural protection of a mountain terrain, flatland–mountain castles required special fortifications such as stone walls, moats, and earthworks. Castles of this type are Hikone Castle in Shiga Prefecture (built in 1606), Himeji Castle in Hyogo Prefecture (built in 1609), Inuyama Castle in Aichi Prefecture (built in 1601 and expanded in 1620), and Hirosaki Castle in Aomori Prefecture (rebuilt in 1810). Kumamoto Castle in Kumamoto Prefecture, Kyushu, has also been rebuilt in this style.

Flatland castles (*hirajiro*) were erected on plains where surrounding castle towns could be built to serve as administrative centers. Thus, political and economic considerations took precedence over defense in their construction. An example is Matsumoto Castle in Nagano Prefecture (built in 1596). Technically, Nijō Castle in Kyoto, built by Tokugawa Ieyasu around 1602, is a flatland castle, though it is really more like a well-fortified villa. Ninomaru Palace and the garden were added in 1626, on the occasion of a visit by the emperor. Although the donjon is gone, the palace still exists – a rare example of Edo Period palace architecture.

Water castles (*mizushiro*) jut out into a body of water. Several, such as Azuchi Castle, erected by Oda Nobunaga in 1579, were built around Lake Biwa, the largest lake in Japan.

Castle Construction

The most important part of a castle was the multi-storied building (donjon) where the lord and his retainers lived. The donjon, which originated in the watchtower constructed on top of a samurai residence, was framed in wood, like most other forms of Japanese architecture. Originally the wood was exposed, but

Large and small connected donjons on one corner of the central enclosure.

A donjon and a connected turret on one corner.

A donjon inside the enclosure.

A main donjon and subsidiary donjons on the inside corner of a secondary enclosure.

Above: The main donjon of a castle and associated turrets could be arranged in a variety of ways. Shown here are some of the most common plans.

Below: Inuyama Castle in Aichi Prefecture. Quite small in comparison to Himeji Castle, its proportions are nevertheless quite elegant.

later the walls were plastered and painted white. Although the plaster and tile protected the donjon from incendiary missiles, they were otherwise rather fragile compared to European castles constructed of stone or brick. In many cases, the castle's primary function was to symbolize the power of the lord and to provide luxurious quarters for living and entertaining. Castles were decorated with screens painted by the most famous artists of the day and featured large *tatami* rooms, often constructed in the Shoin style.

The main defense was provided not by the donjon itself but by the moats, ponds, and walls that created a maze of corridors and courtyards through which attackers had to find their way. If they succeeded in breaching

the castle, they were confronted by a high stone palisade upon which the donjon was constructed. Round, square, and rectangular openings in the walls allowed soldiers to shoot arrows and to fire muskets, as well as to drop rocks and boiling oil or water on their assailants. Both inner and outer walls were reinforced with small towers, similar in design to the donjon, and there were several entrances to provide multiple avenues of escape when necessary. Some castles, such as Himeji and Osaka, were truly formidable. Even the most formidable, however, could be taken by a determined and powerful foe. Osaka Castle, for example, was repeatedly conquered and rebuilt over the centuries.

Decline of Castle Culture

The Edo Period, with the consolidation of power under the Tokugawa shogunate, saw the decline of castle culture. Castles continued to exist but they served as symbols of authority rather than as defensive structures. The first Tokugawa shogun, Tokugawa Ieyasu, decreed that each province should have only one castle to serve as the locus of power for the local warlord (*daimyo*). This meant that many castles had to be dismantled and some new ones built. Though the policy made sense in terms of consolidating and maintaining centralized rule, it led to the destruction of many priceless structures from earlier periods.

Those castles that were fortunate enough to survive Tokugawa policy were not necessarily destined to survive neglect. Some fell into disrepair or were actively dismantled in later periods. Others, such as Matsumoto Castle, have survived against formidable odds. The oldest fully developed castle still in

Himeji Castle

Himeji Castle, widely acclaimed as the most beautiful castle in Japan, evolved from a fort built by the ruler of Harima in 1333. In 1581, Toyotomi Hideyoshi remodeled the fort into a castle, to be used as a base for conducting war against enemies in the western part of the country. In 1601, Ikeda Terumasa, Tokugawa Ieyasu's son-in-law, moved into the castle and spent the next eight years replacing the original donjon with the present buildings and enlarging the castle grounds with its three moats. Research has shown that some of the material from Hideyoshi's original building was used in the present structure. Himeji Castle was designated a World Heritage Site in 1993.

Partly due to its graceful proportions, the size of Himeji Castle is not apparent from a photograph. Some perspective on the monumental proportions of the castle is provided by one of the authors who is standing at the base of the stone foundation (right) upon which the donjon is erected.

Dimly lit interior of one of the five stories of Himeji Castle. Four corridors surround an empty core in the middle. Ceilings are supported by a system of massive posts and beams.

Layout of Himeji Castle. The castle is situated on a hill, steep at the back and sloping toward the surrounding plain in front. The sloping area is protected by multiple walls and moats. Only one moat remains today. Drawing based on a model at the Himeji Castle Museum.

Recently restored, Osaka Castle houses artifacts and displays pertaining to Toyotomi Hideyoshi and his military conquests. Although the concrete structure is smaller than the original, it is nevertheless quite impressive.

Detail of dormers at Osaka Castle. Under the curved roof overhangs are elaborate gable ornaments that frame the rectangular barred windows.

The original stone walls and donjon foundations at Osaka Castle demonstrate the precision with which rocks, some very large, were cut and fitted together.

Osaka Castle

Osaka Castle was built by Hideyoshi in 1583 on the ruins of Ishiyama Honganji, headquarters of the Ikkō sect of Jōdo Shinshū Buddhism. It was burned in battle against the Tokugawa in 1615, rebuilt in 1625, but burned again by retreating loyalists when the Tokugawa shogunate fell in the Meiji Restoration of 1868. The present keep was erected in 1931, damaged during the war, and recently restored. Original structures remaining at Osaka Castle include the Ōtemon Gate, five turrets constructed on different sections of the original stone walls, several arsenals, and a well house. The largest stone used in the walls is over 59 square meters and weighs 130 tons. The 70–90 meter-wide moats and 20-meter-high walls provide some indication of the massive scale of the original castle. The castle is set in a park filled with trees.

existence, Matsumoto Castle was reconstructed at the end of the sixteenth century. The marked contrast between the blackened wood and white plaster used in constructing the walls makes it one of the most striking and beautiful castles in Japan.

The Meiji Restoration of 1868 ushered in a fascination with things Western and a desire to destroy anything associated with Japan's feudal past. The samurai class was abolished, as were many aspects of samurai culture, including castles. Matsumoto Castle was sold for a pittance, to be demolished for its metal parts. Fortunately, however, influential local families raised enough money to buy back and repair the castle. The restored edifice was designated a Historic Site in 1930 and a National Treasure in 1936. Today, it is the main tourist attraction for the city of Matsumoto and the surrounding area.

Opposite: The donjon of Osaka Castle, originally constructed in 1589 and repeatedly rebuilt.

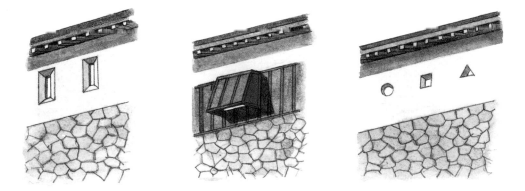

Left: Loopholes, stonedrops, and arrowports in the outer walls and walls of the donjon allowed a variety of missiles to be directed at the enemy.

Centralized Feudalism

Tokugawa Ieyasu completed the unification of Japan, established a system of centralized feudalism, and moved his military capital to Edo (later renamed Tokyo) to begin 250 years of relative peace and isolation. Samurai were at the top of the social hierarchy, but merchants eventually gained control of the wealth, and for the first time in Japanese history common people became the leaders of new cultural developments.

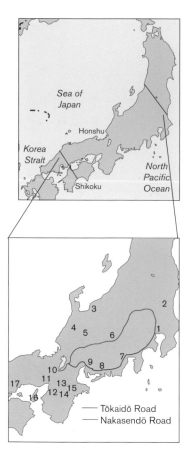

— Tōkaidō Road
— Nakasendō Road

1 Edo
2 Nikkō
3 Kawakami Family House (Toyama)
4 Ogimachi Village
5 Takayama
6 Tsumago and Magome Post Towns
7 Kunōsan Shrine (Shizuoka)
8 Yoshida Post Town
9 Narumi Post Town
10 Kyoto
11 Osaka
12 Yoshimura Family House
   (Habikino City, Osaka Prefecture)
13 Nara
14 Asuka
15 Murōji
16 Awaji Island
17 Kurashiki

History

The Edo (Tokugawa) Period (1600–1868) is not easily divisible into political epochs. In general, the first three Tokugawa shoguns, beginning with Tokugawa Ieyasu, formulated the basic policies of the new regime, designed to end the bloodshed that had characterized Japanese society for so long. To accomplish this goal, they espoused a combination of *bushidō* (Way of the Warrior) and Confucian philosophy that provided an ideological basis for a strict social class system, with *bushi* (samurai) at the top, followed by farmers, artisans, and merchants. Merchants were ranked at the bottom because they were viewed as a non-productive class.

The Tokugawa shogunate took a variety of measures to ensure control, such as assuming ownership of one-fourth of the land, directly ruling most of the major cities, and establishing a hostage system in which *daimyo* (feudal lords) were required to leave their families in Edo. Because they had to pay homage to the shogun every one or two years, *daimyo* spent much of their time and wealth maintaining residences in the capital and traveling to and from their own domains. Uprisings were ruthlessly put down.

After the death of the third Tokugawa shogun, Iemitsu, the shogunate became increasingly conservative. Strapped for cash and faced with increasing discontent from farmers and distant clans, the Edo regime became more or less irrelevant to the expanding mercantile class upon which it had become financially dependent. Many people, including a number of intellectuals, were increasingly concerned that Japan was falling behind the industrialized nations and desired to renew contact with the outside world. Faced with a show of force from the West, symbolized by the visit of Commodore Perry's gunboats in 1853, the feudal structure eventually toppled, ushering in the Meiji Restoration of 1868. The emperor was returned to power, the samurai class was abolished, and Japan began to industrialize as quickly as possible in an attempt to prevent being colonized.

Other Cities in the Edo Period

In addition to Edo, one of the largest cities in the world by the eighteenth century, there were other major cities. Kyoto, which remained the imperial capital, had a population of around 410,000 in 1634. It was known for the production of high quality arts and crafts. In the latter part of the Edo Period, when average people were allowed to travel more freely, Kyoto became a major tourist destination.

Osaka, which had a similar sized population, was an industrial city where many products necessary for daily life, including clothing, metal products, oil, *saké*, and medicine, were produced from raw materials imported from other parts of Japan. Osaka also was the "kitchen" for the entire country. Products such as rice were brought to Osaka by boat from all parts of Japan, and products such as sugar and salt were imported from western Japan. As a result, Osaka became a major port as well as a financial center.

Regional Towns

Centralized feudalism gave rise to several new developments that had a direct bearing upon the architecture of the period. For example, post towns grew up along the major routes leading to the capital. The most famous of these routes was the Tōkaidō, one of the main roads between Kyoto and Edo. Post towns, most of which were small, were spaced to provide overnight lodging for the *daimyo* and their retainers as they traveled to and from Edo. The shogunate helped maintain these post towns and set up *honjin* (officially appointed inns) and horse stables for *daimyo*, aristocrats, and high-ranking priests.

There also were other classes of inns such as *waki-honjin* for lower-ranking people of importance and *hatagoya* for ordinary people. At the bottom of the ladder were inns in which guests had to do their own cooking. Post towns, such as Tsumago and Magome on the old Nakasendō Road, still preserve their Edo Period buildings and are popular tourist destinations.

Castle towns, such as Kanazawa, were created to serve the needs of the lord of the area, and zoning regulations reflected the priority placed upon protection of the castle. Samurai quarters usually were created around the castle; the next area inside the town limits was set aside for *machiya* (merchant shops with living quarters); and the third area consisted of temples. Quarters for the underprivileged, such as "untouchables" and beggars, were set aside outside the city limits, as were the pleasure quarters. In time of war, these outer "rings of defense" were frequently burned, either by the enemy or by the lord himself, who usually had little concern for the welfare of commoners in his area.

Other types of towns included regional administrative centers such as Takayama, which served as headquarters for shogunal representatives; port towns such as Sakai and Nagasaki; towns such as Uji and Yamada that developed around famous temples and shrines; and mining towns such as Aikawa.

In addition to castles, samurai houses, and administrative buildings, these regional metropolitan centers produced a new *chōnin* (townspeople) culture, dominated by businessmen's houses, shops, and factories. A characteristic feature of regional towns was the proliferation of *kura* (storehouses) – separate fireproof buildings for protecting the treasures of the moneyed classes, who spent their free time in the pursuit of pleasure.

Rural Villages

In an attempt to control rural areas, as well as the large cities and provincial towns, the Tokugawa shogunate established a hierarchical system in which farmers who owned property

were responsible for ensuring the payment of taxes, in rice, based upon the amount of fertile land available to a village. One of these influential farmers was appointed village headman. Those without land worked for landowners and had few rights.

Eventually, many rural residents moved into occupations other than farming, either on a part-time or full-time basis. This included the manufacture or sale of items such as fertilizer, *saké*, *miso* (fermented bean paste), soy sauce, vegetables, flour, and firewood. Partly as a result of diversification and increased income, farmhouses became larger than in previous periods and construction techniques became more sophisticated. The most common arrangement was to have a large living area with a sunken fireplace in the front of the house and sleeping and kitchen areas in the rear. Some farmers became wealthy enough to build themselves luxurious homes that incorporated Shoin style features favored by the upper classes in towns and cities. There was, of course, considerable variation in building styles, depending upon the area of the country.

Above: Woodblock print by Hiroshige depicting Narumi Post Town on the Tōkaidō Road. Both buildings use *sangawara buki* tiles.

Below: Basic tile types: *hongawara buki* (a round tile fitting tightly over the seam between two slightly curved pieces); and *sangawara buki* (rounded and curved portions integrated for greater strength).

Left: This mid-Edo townhouse (the former Kawakami family house) is the oldest extant *machiya* in Toyama Prefecture.

Edo: The Feudal Capital

Right: Detail from a seventeenth-century screen at the National Museum of Japanese History, depicting the main donjon of the castle and part of the surrounding palace (Honmaru) area where the shogun lived. Palace buildings were similar to the extant Ninomaru Palace on the grounds of Nijō Castle in Kyoto.

Below: "Edo Nihonbashi," a woodblock print from Hokusai's "36 views of Mount Fuji" series, depicts the Nihonbashi bridge area of Edo. Built in 1603, Nihonbashi was the center not only of Edo but also of Japan as a whole. The five official roads of Japan (Tōkaidō, Nakasendō, Nikkō-dōchū, Ōshū-dōchū, and Kōshū-dōchū) all start here. The warehouses shown in the picture belonged to wholesalers of Japanese cypress lumber. Edo Castle and Mount Fuji can both be seen in the distance.

Edo, the military capital of the Togugawa shoguns for approximately 250 years, was often destroyed by fire, but it always bounced back. By the end of the seventeenth century, Edo was one of the largest cities in the world and the center of a burgeoning merchant class that had a major impact upon Japanese culture.

History

There are different opinions as to the exact location of the original Edo, which many consider to mean "mouth of the bay." Its strategic location prompted a samurai, Edo Shirō Shigetsugu, to build his villa, Edo Yakata, there in the twelth century (Kamakura Period). In 1457, Ōta Dōkan, a high-ranking retainer of a local lord, built Edo Castle on the site of Edo Yakata. The castle changed hands several times after Dōkan was murdered in 1486.

Tokugawa Ieyasu moved into the castle in 1590 while he was still a subordinate of the great military ruler Toyotomi Hideyoshi. Ieyasu must have recognized the geographical advantages of the location, even though the castle itself was not sufficiently grand to serve as the residence of a lord who aspired to rule the entire country, and the city was not well developed. Ieyasu took on the task of developing Edo as soon as he moved there. The first project was to dig a canal from the bay to the castle for bringing in materials needed to re-build the castle, as well as making moats around the castle. Edo Castle was the largest in the world, with an outer wall 16 kilometers long and 5 meters thick, breached by 11 gates. A maze of inner moats and walls made it virtually impregnable.

After Ieyasu became shogun in 1603, he took on a more ambitious plan for developing Edo. He cut down mountains and moved the dirt to fill in the bay, requiring *daimyo* to supply the necessary labor force. Major land routes, such as Tōkaidō and Nakasendō, for bringing goods to Edo were established. Some say that these roads were designed to provide the best views of Mount Fuji and Mount Tsukuba, as well as Edo Castle, but more practical considerations, such as the location of existing roads and rivers, probably predominated. The center part of Edo was based on the grid layout of Kyoto, an urban design feature that originally came from Tang Dynasty China in the Nara Period.

The enormous project came to completion in 1637 when the third Tokugawa shogun, Iemitsu, completed the rebuilding of Edo Castle and the surrounding Honmaru District. *Edo-zu Byōbu* (screen paintings of scenes in Edo) depict vivid views of early Edo, such as the castle, samurai houses surrounding it, *machiya*, and temples. The rapid increase in the population of Edo was largely due to the introduction of the *sankin-kōtai* (alternate attendance) system, which required all *daimyo* to spend some time in Edo, and to leave their families there as hostages, accompanied by their retainers and servants. As the number of *daimyo* and samurai households increased, more and more average citizens moved to Edo to provide them with basic goods and services.

A disastrous fire in 1657, which left 60 percent of Edo (including Edo Castle) in ashes and around 100,000 people dead, prompted the feudal government to make maps of the area and develop an ambitious rebuilding plan to disperse buildings and develop new housing areas – measures designed to help prevent the spread of fire.

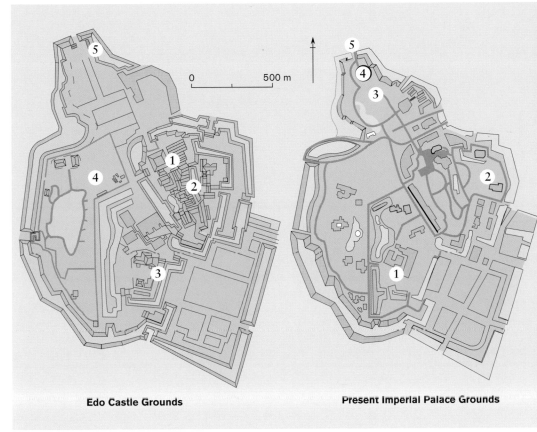

Edo Castle Grounds

Present Imperial Palace Grounds

Edo Castle

After the Meiji Restoration of 1868, the emperor moved from Kyoto to Edo. A new Imperial Palace built in 1888 was destroyed during World War II. The present palace complex was completed in 1968.

Edo Castle Grounds

1 Castle Donjon
2 Honmaru (shogun's palace)
3 Nishi-no-maru (West Enclosure): additional palace building
4 Fukiage Garden with pond (firebreak)
5 Tayasumon Gate

Present Imperial Palace Grounds

1 New Palace
2 East Garden (open to the public)
3 Kita-no-maru Park (open to the public)
4 Nihon Budōkan (Japan Martial Arts Hall)
5 Tayasumon Gate

The New Edo

Edo Castle was partially rebuilt and the city of Edo greatly expanded. It is estimated that by 1693 there were 350,000 commoners and 600,000–700,000 samurai, making Edo larger than either London or Paris. Some of the newly rich members of the merchant class built large dwellings with a third story in the early part of the Edo Period, but these were prohibited later when the government issued an order directing commoners to refrain from such extravagance. Commoners were allowed, even encouraged, however, to build houses with tiled roofs and fireproof storehouses (*kura*). Tiled roofs had become less costly and more fireproof after *sangawara* tiles, described earlier, were invented. As a result, *kura* were built everywhere, partly as status symbols.

Edo Culture

Eventually, Edo developed its own distinctive *ukiyo* (floating world). This was a hedonistic culture that catered to the whims of an increasingly wealthy business class which, deprived of political power and status, spent its time and money pursuing sensual pleasures. Life in the Yoshiwara pleasure district of Edo was frequently the subject of *ukiyo-e*, paintings and woodblock prints that depicted beautiful courtesans and Kabuki actors.

Edo produced little in the way of distinctive architecture, apart from the grandeur of its original castle. The Tokugawa shogunate left its mark on Japanese architecture, however, with the building of the mausoleums at Nikkō, which serve as memorials to the first and third shoguns. These baroque shrines are suitable symbols of the aesthetic taste of the feudal rulers, who preferred ostentation over the aesthetic refinement of the imperial court, which continued to exist in the official capital of Kyoto until the Meiji Restoration of 1868, when the emperor was restored to power and the imperial capital was moved to Edo.

Despite measures taken to prevent the spread of fire, described above, more than 90 serious fires and the Great Kanto Earthquake of 1923 repeatedly destroyed the capital. This tragic loss was repeated in World War II when firebombing reduced the city to rubble. As a result, very little of the original architecture from the Edo Period remains.

Takayama: An Administrative Town

In the Nara Period, the villages of Hida (present-day Gifu Prefecture) were unable to pay taxes because of poor rice yields. In place of taxes, each village was required to send ten artisans to Nara to help construct the new capital. As a result, Hida carpenters became renowned for their skill. Their handiwork is preserved in the old provincial town of Takayama, a bustling city that combines the old and the new. Takayama has had the foresight to preserve a large area of traditional architecture known as the Sanmachi District, which attracts millions of visitors each year who come to see its traditional houses, shops, *saké* breweries, and temples.

History of Takayama

Provincial domains were under the control of local *daimyo*, who owed fealty to the shogun in Edo but who otherwise retained a good deal of local autonomy. In some cases, however, particular districts, including the large cities, were considered too important, because of their strategic location or resources, to be left in the hands of *daimyo*, and came under the direct administrative control of a governor appointed by the shogun. These special districts were called *tenryō* and the buildings in which administrative activities were conducted were known as *jinya*. Although there were 60 *jinya* and sub-*jinya* in the Edo Period, Takayama Jinya is the only one remaining today.

According to local legends, when Minamoto Yoritomo destroyed the Taira clan and set himself up in Kamakura as Japan's first military shogun, surviving members of the defeated Taira clan escaped to the Hida District, where some settled in Takayama. It is said that they were attracted to Takayama because it resembled Kyoto, their home, with its mountain setting and rivers running through. Takayama came to be known as "Little Kyoto."

In the sixteenth century, Takayama became the headquarters of Kanamori Nagachika, a general who served under Japan's military ruler, Toyotomi Hideyoshi. In accordance with Chinese principles of geomancy, Kanamori's castle was built on a rise between two rivers, with a hill to the north and a concentration of shrines and temples to the northeast to provide protection. The Kanamori family ruled for six generations, during which time the political, economic, and cultural infrastructure was put in place for a thriving metropolis, and Takayama became the area's administrative center.

In 1692, the shogun, desiring the timber and mineral resources of the area for himself, took direct control of Takayama and sent the Kanamori family to Tohoku (northeast part of Japan). The castle was demolished and the former villa of the daughter of the third head of the Kanamori clan was remodeled into the office (*jinya*) of the new governor, Ina Henjūrō Tadaatsu. Tadaatsu and his 24 successors were Edo urbanites and thus men of taste. Because their real passion was traditional culture rather than politics, Takayama became well known for its arts and crafts. It remained the provincial administrative center of the Hida District until the Meiji Restoration of 1868.

Above: Cutout picture (*kiri-e*) by Yoshimoto Norihito, a contemporary artist, depicting a famous intersection in the old Sanmachi District of Takayama.

Right: Originally constructed in 1615, Takayama's administrative building (*jinya*) was remodeled in 1816. Resembling a small-scale palace, the buildings of the *jinya* are enclosed by high walls, entered through an impressive gate.

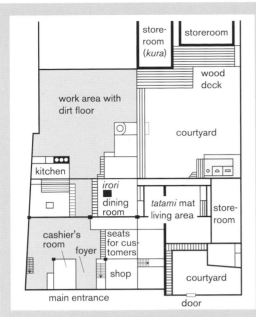

Room layout of the interior of the Yoshijima house. The *saké* shop and cashier's room, as well as the kitchen and foyer, occupy the front area of the house, covered by the massive roof beams. *Kura* (storerooms) and living quarters of the family occupy the back half of the house. Rooms are arranged around two courtyards.

(Floor plan labels: storeroom (*kura*), storeroom, work area with dirt floor, wood deck, courtyard, kitchen, *irori*, dining room, *tatami* mat living area, storeroom, cashier's room, foyer, seats for customers, shop, courtyard, main entrance, door)

Yoshijima House

The dark vertical wooden slats covering much of the building are balanced by the white *shōji* and the tan stucco areas, some of which have a strong horizontal orientation. From outside, it appears that the building has two stories. There is, however, only one story adjacent to the street, the upper portion of which is occupied by the roof beams. This compromise provided the house with an air of magnificence, while complying with the Edo regulation that merchant houses could not have more than one floor facing the street. The back of the house, where the family lived, had two sumptuously appointed stories that reflected the family's wealth.

Dining room of the Yoshijima house, with an *irori* (sunken hearth) for boiling water.

Wood-fired stove made of bricks in the kitchen of the Yoshijima house.

Merchants of Takayama

As the administrative center of the district, Takayama attracted many people, such as merchants and artisans, and soon developed into the largest and most prosperous city in the district. Many of the newcomers started their own businesses, making products such as *saké* and *miso*, selling rice and tobacco, and lending money. Some of these families, such as the Kusakabe and Yoshijima, prospered and before long the wealth of the Hida District was concentrated in the hands of a small number of merchant families who used much of their newfound riches to enhance the cultural and artistic activities sponsored by the town's administrators. In other words, despite the fact that merchants ranked lower than artisans and farmers in terms of the neo-Confucian ideology espoused by the Edo shogunate, government officials and merchants became financially and socially interdependent.

Merchant Houses

Despite the wealth and influence of the large merchant families, the official ranking system had to be maintained. Thus, houses near the center of the city were not allowed to have a second story, to prevent inhabitants from looking down on the *jinya*, or upon samurai on the streets below. This did not prevent wealthy merchants from displaying their wealth by constructing mansions that had only one floor but sported massive roofs supported by an elaborate system of posts and beams. Typical of this kind of large merchant house (*machiya*) is the Yoshijima residence, which dates from the mid-Edo period.

The Yoshijima family came to Takayama in 1784 and has been in the business of making *saké* ever since. Like other wealthy merchants, the Yoshijima family constructed a dwelling in accordance with feudal provisions that regulated the size of merchant houses to ensure that they did not threaten the status of the samurai (*bushi*) class. When the original house burned in 1905 (Meiji Period), it was rebuilt by famous Hida carpenter Nishida Isaburō in a style that more accurately reflected the considerable wealth of the Yoshijima family. The remodeled house maintained a relatively modest external appearance but included a partial second floor with several comfortable rooms. The Yoshijima house is considered one of the best examples of traditional merchant dwellings and has been designated an Important Cultural Property.

Below: Woodblock print by Tosa Mitsuoki depicting carpenters at work.

Left: Interior of an old *machiya* (business-residence), a few of which are well-preserved in Takayama, Kanazawa, Kyoto, and some other towns and cities. Shown here is the tearoom in Kondaya Genbei, an elegant *machiya* in the Muromachi district of Kyoto built in the 1730s. It still serves as a residence and shop where traditional kimonos and *obi* sashes are made and sold. Typically, this tearoom is small (four and a half *tatami* mats) and plain so as not to distract from the important goal of achieving harmony within oneself.

Kanazawa: A Castle Town

Castle towns were administrative, commercial, and cultural centers of the feudal period. Situated on the Japan Sea side, Kanazawa was the castle town of the Maeda clan and Japan's fourth largest city in the Edo Period. Spared saturation bombing in World War II, Kanazawa has more historically important architecture than most cities, as well as one of Japan's three most important gardens, Kenrokuen.

Functions of a Castle Town

During the period of decentralized feudalism (Kamakura, Muromachi, and Momoyama Periods), Japan lacked an effective centralized government. Consequently, local warlords (*daimyo*) set up castles and controlled as much territory as they could defend. *Daimyo* made their own laws, collected taxes, and attempted to develop internal trade, commerce, and culture. Towns quickly grew up around castles to service the needs and aspirations of the *daimyo* and their samurai retainers. Over time, castle towns often became important commercial and cultural centers in their own right. After national unity was established under the Tokugawa shogunate in 1600, most *daimyo* were allowed to continue exercising some control over their domains, but they had to swear fealty to Edo and agree to abide by its restrictions and requirements. As a result of their relative autonomy, provincial towns such as Kanazawa flourished until the demise of the feudal system as a result of the Meiji Restoration of 1868.

Above: Samurai houses situated along one of the old canals that were constructed to bring water to Kenrokuen Garden and the castle.

Opposite above left: Gate and wall of a former samurai house in the Nagamachi District of Kanazawa. Some old gates, such as this one, boast Judas windows, behind which guards were once posted.

Opposite above right: Sanmon Gate of Tentokuin, a Sōtō sect Zen temple in Kanazawa. Tentokuin was established in 1623 by the third Maeda *daimyo*, Toshitsune, for his deceased wife. All of the original buildings were burned in a fire in 1671 except for the Sanmon.

Right: Hishiyagura turret of Kanazawa Castle is equipped with defensive features such as stone drops and slots for firing rifles.

History

In 1546, a Buddhist sect established an autocracy in the Kaga area (the present Ishikawa Prefecture), with its head temple on the site of what later became Kanazawa Castle. The area prospered but eventually was conquered in 1583 by Maeda Toshiie, who took control in the name of Toyotomi Hideyoshi. Maeda's castle was built on a hill between two rivers, and the town of Kanazawa developed around it. After Hideyoshi's death, the Maeda clan allied with Tokugawa Ieyasu and joined the battle of Sekigahara in 1600, in which Ieyasu defeated the last of his enemies to complete the task of unifying Japan. As a result, Maeda Toshiie was rewarded with a domain (including Ishikawa) so large that it is said to have produced 1 million *koku* (more than 5 million US bushels) of rice, making the Maeda clan one of the wealthiest in Japan.

The Maeda clan used its vast income from taxes on rice to patronize the arts and traditional culture. Kanazawa thus became famous for its tea ceremonies, Noh plays, silk cloth, Kutani-yaki ceramics, and other crafts. Kanazawa also had an extensive samurai area, a flourishing entertainment district, replete with geisha houses, and two temple districts. After the destruction of feudalism at the time of the Meiji Restoration, the numerous samurai of Kanazawa found themselves without jobs, and the local artisans and entertainers lost their patrons. As a result, Kanazawa slowly sank into obscurity. Today, Kanazawa has regained some of its former prosperity as a major tourist destination.

Castle Remains

Because of its close ties with Hideyoshi and then the new Tokugawa shogunate, the Maeda castle was never strongly fortified. It was destroyed by fire in 1881, leaving only the Ishikawamon Gate complex (eight buildings, including the rear gate, constructed around an enclosed square) and a Long House, used for the storage of weapons. The gate is roofed with lead tiles, which have weathered white. The Long House, built in 1858, is a two-story construction that stretches for 48 meters on top of the castle's outer wall.

The remaining structures overlook a portion of the moat that has been filled in for use as a road. Nearby is the *daimyo*'s private strolling park, now known as Kenrokuen, generally acknowledged to be one of the three most beautiful gardens in Japan.

Samurai and Entertainment Districts

Located near Kanazawa Castle, the Nagamachi area preserves the twisting, dead-end streets and canals of the Edo Period, constructed to repel invasions. The samurai houses of the area were surrounded by high mud walls and formal gates, the sizes of which were determined by the status of the family. Today, many of the samurai houses have been replaced by modern houses that retain the old samurai gates.

Two areas were set aside by the Kaga area feudal government as entertainment quarters during the Edo Period. At Higashi Chaya-Machi, one of these two areas, the streets are still lined with houses, each with their *kōshi* (lattice) windows and colorfully painted interior walls. In the Edo Period, these quarters were crowded with samurai and wealthy businessmen who came to watch highly cultivated geishas perform the traditional arts, such as singing, dancing, reciting poetry, and playing the *koto* (Japanese harp) and *shamisen* (three-stringed instrument).

Temple and Merchant Districts

All castle towns have at least one temple quarter, situated to provide a first line of defense against invasion. Kanazawa has two temple areas: Teramachi, with 70 temples situated on the Saigawa River on the west side of the city, and Utatsuyama, with 50 temples situated on the Asanogawa River on the east side of the city. The main thoroughfares of the city were lined with retail shops, and the back streets housed the artisans, with the various trades assigned to areas with names such as the Saltsellers' District and Metalworkers' District. Today, Kanazawa is once again a flourishing craft center, famous for its lacquerware, woodcarvings, woodblock prints, and utensils covered with silver and gold. It is also known for its *saké* and fermented soy bean products.

Kenrokuen Garden and Seisonkaku Villa

Kenrokuen, one of the three most famous gardens in Japan, is organized around a large pond fed by water brought many kilometers by tunnels and canals. It is attached to Seisonkaku, a sumptuous villa constructed for the mother of the thirteenth Maeda lord (see pages 140–1). Reflecting the power of the Maeda family, Seisonkaku has walls covered with gold leaf and lacquered beams.

Below: Woodblock print by Edo Period artist Toyonobu depicting the interior of a geisha house. Geisha houses, euphemistically known as "teahouses," were found in the "floating world" districts of major cities and important regional towns such as Kanazawa.

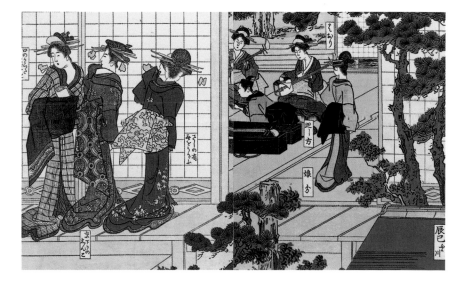

Ogimachi: A Farm Village

Above: A Gasshō style house in the village of Ogimachi.

Pages 116–17: Gasshō style houses in the mountainous Shirakawagō area of Gifu Prefecture, nestle in a valley below towering mountains.

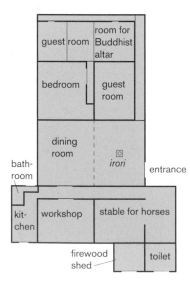

Above: Additional rooms are often added to the basic plan of the Gasshō style house.

The houses in Ogimachi farm village have steep thatched roofs known as Gasshō ("hands folded in prayer") style. Spread along the Shōgawa River deep in the mountains of Gifu Prefecture, Ogimachi Village has a tradition going back hundreds of years. At one time, most Japanese farmhouses were thatched, but today there are very few such buildings left.

History of Ogimachi

Although people have been living in this area, known as Shirakawa-gō, since the late Jōmon Period, about 10,000 years ago, little is known about life in Ogimachi prior to the twelfth century. In the fifteenth century, the Uchigashima clan invaded the area and built a castle, which no longer exists, on a hill at the edge of Ogimachi. The Edo shogunate assumed direct control of Ogimachi in the seventeenth century, but part of the territory remained under the control of the Jōdo-Shin Buddhist temple, Shōrenji.

Prior to 1600, there were about 50 houses in the village, but by the mid-Meiji Period, that number had increased to over 100. After the Meiji government built a national highway through the village in 1890, modern houses were built along the highway. Today, Ogimachi has 113 Gasshō style buildings mixed with 329 modern buildings, two Buddhist temples, two Shinto shrines, and miscellaneous other buildings. The modern buildings are regulated in size and construction so as not to clash with the traditional architecture.

When the famous German architect Bruno Taut visited the Tōyama family house in the Shirakawa-gō area in 1935, he found 36 people living in the building. Because of a scarcity of flat and usable land, the Gasshō style houses were built large enough to accommodate an extended family, typically consisting of grandparents, parents, unmarried children, the eldest son with his wife and children, and married daughters with their children. Husbands of married daughters remained with their own families. Only the eldest son was allowed to bring his wife to live with his parents.

In late feudal times, villagers made gunpowder the old-fashioned way – pouring urine over mineral ingredients stored under the porches. With the advent of commercial gunpowder, the villagers switched to raising silkworms to supplement their income from rice, which was meager due to the poor soil in this mountainous area. Silkworms were raised on the top floor where they were kept warm by heat and smoke rising from an open fire pit on the first floor.

When the Shōgawa River was damned, a number of Gasshō style buildings were moved to Minkaen, an open-air museum with 25 Gasshō style houses adjacent to Ogimachi Village. Today, the village has an active society dedicated to preserving the remaining Gasshō style buildings. In 1995, their efforts were recognized by UNESCO, which designated Ogimachi a World Heritage Site. Today, more than 600 people still live in the village. Although there are several *minshuku* (bed-and-breakfast establishments), private houses are occupied by their owners and thus are not normally open to the general public.

Difficulties of Preservation

Preserving these large thatched farmhouses is difficult because of deep snow and the ever-present threat of fire. In the old days, it was not uncommon for 1.5 meters of snow to accumulate on the massive roofs. Although there is less snow today, the roofs still have to be cleared on a regular basis to avoid collapse.

Thatched roofs are also susceptible to decay and infestation by insects and rodents. Both conditions are kept in check by the use of a fire built on the first floor for heating and cooking. A rectangular slatted grate (*hiama*) is hung over the fire pit to catch sparks from the open fire and to diffuse heat and smoke. Smoke from the fire rises through the *hiama* and spaced flooring on the upper stories to infiltrate the roof. The village has regular fire drills in which streams of water are sprayed on the houses from hydrants throughout the town site.

Physical Layout

All but two of the Gasshō style houses face north and south. This allows the large sloped roofs to catch the maximum amount of sun, essential for keeping the thatch dry, and reduces exposure to the winds that blow north and south along the river. The toilet is at one end of the house and the Buddhist altar is at the other end, next to the wall, so it can easily be removed in case of fire. The placement of the toilet and altar in adjacent houses is reversed so that the toilet of one house never faces the altar of the next. On the first floor, the main room is a large open area featuring an open hearth (*irori*), where wood is burned to heat the house, keep a hanging tea kettle hot, and smoke food items.

Structure of a Gasshō Style House

Gasshō means "praying hands." The term refers to the steep slope of the roofs, which are designed to shed the heavy snows and rains typical of the region. Three to five stories, these large farmhouses formerly accommodated extended families. Roof timbers are tied together with straw rope and the lower part of the structure is secured with wooden pins. Houses in Ogimachi Village are inhabited and thus not normally open to the public. On the edge of the village, however, is an outstanding open-air museum consisting of 25 Gasshō style buildings that have been moved from nearby villages. The photographs shown here are from different buildings.

Beams used in the roof are tied together with straw ropes. This provides both strength and flexibility when there are heavy snow loads, high winds, or earthquakes.

The structure of the top floor, where silkworms were traditionally raised by members of the extended family, allowed variations in light, air, and heat at different stages of cultivation.

Miscanthus grass, a type of pampas, is stored under the eaves of a shed to keep it dry in readiness for thatching. The roof thatch can be up to 1 meter thick.

Smoke from the open hearth rises through slats in the ceiling, protecting the thatch against insects and dampness.

The main entrance is normally on the side rather than the gable end.

Roof rafters projecting through the gable end support the large overhang. The roofs typically slope at around 60 degrees.

Replacing the Roof

When properly cared for, thatched roofs last for around 100 years. Many of the houses are at least 250 years old; some have been owned by the same families for many generations. Replacing a roof is a community effort carried out by a labor-sharing system called *yui*. *Yui* provides labor not only for repairing houses, especially roofs, but also for activities such as planting, harvesting, and clearing snow.

It takes several months to collect and dry the grass for a new roof, tie it into bundles, and organize a workforce of several hundred people. When preparations are complete, it takes three days to remove the old thatch, and about one day to replace any roof timbers that have decayed, tie on the new bundles of grass, and trim the thatch. At any one time, as many as 100 people may be working on the roof, with several times that number of people on the ground tying grass bundles and engaged in support activities such as preparing food.

Left: A smoke-darkened roof after the old thatch has been removed in preparation for rethatching.

Opposite: A roof being re-thatched. About 100 people are on the roof of the house, with 300–400 more working inside or on the ground.

Below: The steps in constructing a Gasshō style roof.

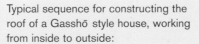

Typical sequence for constructing the roof of a Gasshō style house, working from inside to outside:

1 Large rafters are attached to the ridgepole.
2 Horizontal beams are placed across the rafters at right angles.
3 Small rafters are used to create a grid between the large rafters.
4 The exterior surface is covered with reed mats.
5 Thatch bundles are placed over the reed mats and tied to the roof frame with vines inserted through the mats.

Finally, on the inside:

6 Large beams, to which the floor is attached, are tied to the large rafters at each floor level.
7 Diagonal poles are attached to the large rafters on the inside of each roof slope.
8 Large cross beams, parallel to the floor, connect the two roof slopes on the top floor.

No nails are used in the process. The roof frame is tied together with rope, and the thatch bundles are attached to the frame with vines. Because no metal is used, the roofs are ecologically sound, especially since the old thatch is burned as fuel when the roof is redone.

Unfortunately, the cost of replacing a roof is becoming prohibitive – up to half a million US dollars. Moreover, the pampas grass used for thatching is becoming difficult to find in sufficient quantities. As a result, some families can no longer continue the rethatching tradition and are being forced to replace, or cover, the thatch with tin.

Because the houses are made of wood and thatch, they are extremely vulnerable to fire. As a consequence, there are numerous fire drills in which houses are sprayed with giant streams of water – a tourist attraction in its own right. In the evenings, volunteers patrol the streets, urging Ogimachi residents to be careful with the use of fire.

Overleaf: Ogimachi, located on the steep mountains of Japan's Chubu area, receives some of the heaviest snowfalls in Japan, up to 13 feet (4 meters) a year. The large thatched roofs, steeply sloped in the *gasshō* style, help reduce the weight of the heavy snow.

Minka: Rural Houses

Above: The former Yamashita residence from Fukui Prefecture is an Ō-uragata style farmhouse with thick pillars and beams to withstand the heavy snowfall in the area. The house has been moved to the Open-air Museum of Old Japanese Farmhouses in Osaka.

Opposite: Roughly hewn beech beams and polished zelkova posts are connected together with notched joints in this 180-year-old *minka* in mountainous Niigata Prefecture, which has been painstakingly restored by German architect Karl Bengs using traditional methods.

Below: Woodblock print by Edo Period artist Tamenobu depicting Ishibe, a post town with farmhouse style shops on the Tōkaidō Road.

In contrast to urban townhouses (*machiya*), rural residences are called *minka* – a term that covers everything from the estates of village headmen to the huts of poor farmers. *Minka* also vary according to region of the country and date of construction. Some *minka*, dating back to the Edo Period, have been remodeled over the years, depending upon the needs of the owners.

Farmhouse Floor Plan and Structure

Farmhouses have their origins in the *tateana* (pit houses) or *heichi jūkyo* (flatland dwellings) of ancient times. The floor area of the oldest type of farmhouse known today was equally divided between a dirt floor and an open raised area constructed of wood. Gradually, the percentage of the living area devoted to the raised portion was increased to provide more space for individual rooms. Until recently, however, most of the time indoors was spent on the dirt floor.

The central area of a farmhouse is known as the *kamiya*, which corresponds to the *moya* of a Buddhist temple. In old farmhouses, numerous posts were used to support the roof. The number of posts was gradually decreased by resting large weight-bearing beams upon widely spaced posts to create a basic structure, on top of which was constructed a complicated network of interlocking vertical and horizontal members, known as the *koya-gumi*, to support the roof. In brief, the living area beneath the main beams was simplified but the roof structure above the main beams was made more complicated. When left open, the *koya-gumi* added to the grandeur and aesthetic appeal of the interior of a traditional farmhouse.

The largest area on the raised floor portion is the living room (*O-ie*), which is frequently bordered by peripheral rooms, also on the raised floor. From the raised floor, one steps down to the dirt floor where the kitchen and other work areas are located. Together, the combination of raised floor and earthen area developed into a simple, functional, and aesthetically pleasing style that provided a marked contrast to urban mansions with their elegant Shoin style rooms.

Regional Variation

Farmhouses all over Japan have a similar basic structure. However, unique styles developed in different parts of Japan, sometimes as adaptations to local climatic and living conditions. Most of the old surviving *minka* belonged to village headmen or other wealthy commoners and are thus not necessarily typical. Nevertheless, they provide valuable information on regional variation.

Gasshō style farmhouses are farmhouses with steep roofs suitable for areas with heavy snow such as Gifu and Toyama Prefectures. Winds bearing precipitation from the mainland hit the Japanese Alps that run down the center of the main island of Honshu and dump their load of snow before crossing the mountains.

Magariya are L-shape houses, found in the Nambu area (Iwate Prefecture) of northeastern Japan, that include a living space for the family, as well as a stable for the animals. In winter, heat from the living area is vented into the stable to help keep the horses warm.

Another northern style is the Kabutoyane (samurai helmet) roof that facilitates windows on its upper floors to provide light during winter when ground floor windows are covered with snow.

U-shaped Kudo style houses in Kyushu may have developed in response to the frequent typhoons that strike southern Japan. With its "back to the wind," the U-shaped roof presumably has an aerodynamic quality that shunts the wind off to both sides.

Other styles do not necessarily have a functional explanation. For example, Honmune style houses found in Nagano Prefecture have a bird-like ornament known as a "sparrow dance" on the roof.

Above: Unfinished logs and bamboo bound with rice straw rope hold Bengs's reconstructed *minka* together, and impart a rugged beauty. A 20 inch (50 cm) thick thatch roof sits atop. Traditionally, lofts were used for raising silkworms or for storage and were accessed via a Japanese staircase chest (*kaidan dansu*) fitted with removable drawers and a closet. In this reconstruction, a staircase has been installed and electric lights brighten up the dark space.

Four Additional Roof Styles

Farmhouses are characterized by a variety of basic shapes and roof styles, some of which can be explained in terms of functional considerations. Two of these, the Gasshō and Ō-uragata styles, have been discussed earlier. Four additional styles are shown here.

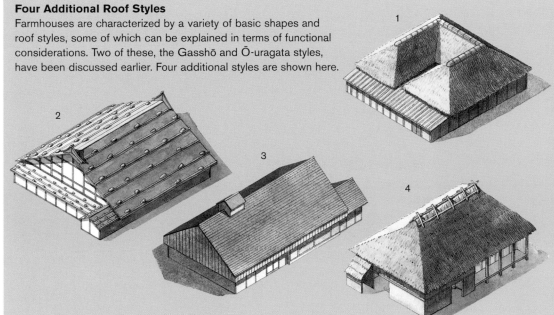

1 Kudo style, Saga Prefecture, with a U-shaped roof.

2 Honmune style, Shinshū area, with a sparrow dance decoration.

3 Totsukawa style, on the border between Wakayama and Nara Prefectures, with a wooden shingle roof and vertical boards under the eaves to protect the building from the heavy rains that occur in the area.

4 Saoya style, Miyazaki Prefecture, with rooms arranged in a row to create narrow buildings suitable for construction on strips of land on mountain slopes.

Thatched Roof Ridges

The steep pitch of traditional Japanese farmhouses was similar throughout the country, due to the need to protect thatch from rain and snow. There was a great deal of variation, however, in the design and structure of roof ridges. In general, roof ridges north of Tokyo were simpler than those to the south, where they sometimes received elaborate treatment.

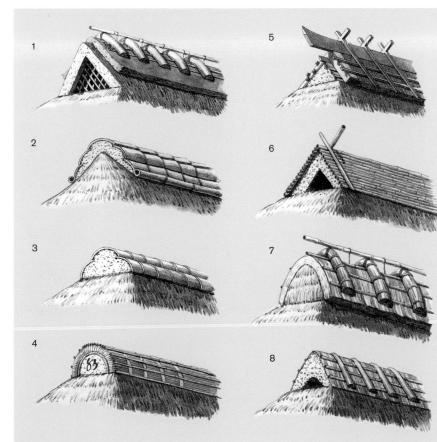

1 Thatched ridge and thick thatch saddles sheathed with bark are held in place with bamboo poles.

2 Tiles are embedded in a layer of clay and chopped straw. Bamboo poles hold the lower tiles in place.

3 Curved tiles on either side of the ridge are capped with similar tiles placed on the crest.

4 Ridge is covered with small bamboo poles, topped with bark strips bent over the crest and longitudinal bamboo poles.

5 Ridge is capped with a sturdy wooden supplemental roof derived from temple architecture.

6 Ridge is covered with a sheath of bamboo. Rafter poles at the ends project through the thatch.

7 Ridge is covered with strips of bark, held in place with bamboo poles, and cylindrical straw saddles.

8 Similar construction to 7, but the straw saddles are sheathed with bark, and small smoke holes are left.

Left: The wood-floored living room in this restored 1912 *minka* is a remodeled *tatami* room. The owner, graphic designer Yamamoto Takeshi, applied the fresh raw lacquer to the floor himself. The structure and exterior of the house have been left unchanged apart from refitting new roof tiles and re-finishing the stucco walls, but some twenty-first century comforts have been added inside without compromising the integrity of the original building.

Yoshimura House

The Yoshimura House in Habikino City, Osaka Prefecture, built around 1615, is one of the oldest extant farmhouses in Japan. In 1937, it was designated a National Treasure, the first *minka* to receive that honor. In 1975, the entire compound was redesignated an Important Cultural Property. The original ancestor of the Yoshimura family settled in this area in the early Kamakura Period. He became the most powerful headman in the district, eventually governing 18 farm villages.

The Yoshimura compound is surrounded by an earthen wall, entered through a large *nagaya-mon* gate that incorporates rooms for guards, servants, and storage. This large structure, covered with a hipped-and-gable thatched roof, was a sign of status granted only to a few commoners. The main building, like most *minka*, is divided into an earth-floored area, where work such as processing and cooking food was done, and an elevated area covered with *tatami* mats. The raised area, parts of which are separated from the courtyard by verandas, is divided into several rooms for living, dining, sleeping, and entertaining. A large guest room at one end is an early example of how the Shoin style was incorporated from urban mansions into the homes of upper-class farmers. It has its own recessed alcove, as well as a built-in desk that overlooks a covered corridor.

There is also a raised interior veranda with a wood floor, called the *hiroshiki*, that projects from the *tatami* area into the earth-floored area, to provide a semi-formal transition between work and relaxation areas. Overhead, the large roof is supported by a *koya-gumi* structure, largely concealed by a bamboo ceiling, resting on

rough-hewn beams. When the Yoshimura House was renovated about 200 years ago, the roof was changed to the Yamatomune style seen today — a thatched gable roof with tiled roof extensions.

Most people enter the Yoshimura House through doors that open on the earth-floored area. Important guests, however, use an elaborate entry foyer that opens on the raised portion of the house. In the feudal period, visitors from the samurai class were provided with their own gate to the compound, reserved for members of the ruling class. The present owners of the house are descended from the original Yoshimura headman who constructed the building. The Yoshimura compound is open to the public twice a year, once in the spring and once in the fall.

Above: Yoshimura House, built in the Yamtomune style, with a thatched roof and tiled extensions.

Below: Layout of the Yoshimura House.

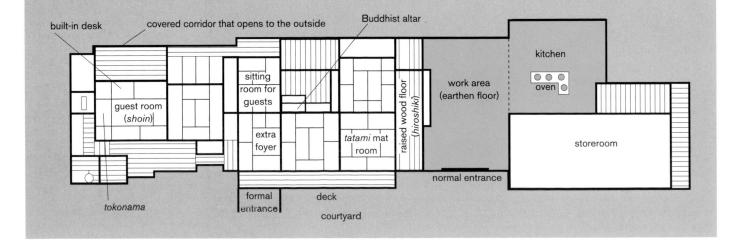

built-in desk   covered corridor that opens to the outside   Buddhist altar

kitchen

oven

sitting room for guests

guest room (*shoin*)

extra foyer

tatami mat room

raised wood floor (*hiroshiki*)

work area (earthen floor)

storeroom

normal entrance

tokonama

formal entrance

deck

courtyard

Farmhouse Reconstructions

Traditional Japanese farmhouses, with their steep thatched roofs, exposed pillars and beams, and sliding panels that can be removed to provide an intimate contact with nature, have a romantic appeal for many people. Farmhouses that have been abandoned or neglected by their owners are being purchased by those who wish to return to their rural roots or who are searching for a more natural lifestyle. Sometimes, these farmhouses are even purchased by foreigners who have developed a love of traditional Japanese houses.

Restoration

In some cases, traditional farmhouses are being restored to their original state – to the extent that structural considerations and local building codes permit. This often involves undoing changes that have been made over the years by successive generations of inhabitants who may have covered the original thatch roof with tin, replaced the open hearth or clay oven with more modern appliances, or replaced sliding panels with permanent walls.

Restoration also may involve replacing pillars and beams that have rotted to the extent that they are no longer safe or aesthetically appealing with members salvaged from an old farmhouse that is being dismantled. Restoring an original thatch roof requires finding large quantities of appropriate reeds. Finding authentic materials and knowledgeable craftspeople is becoming increasingly difficult and expensive. The rewards, however, for those who persevere, are many. Particularly pleasing is the play of light and shadows in a building with a massive roof supported by an open and intricate system of posts and beams, or the patina of wooden hallways and verandas made dark and shiny by years of use.

Modification

In other cases, traditional farmhouses are being modified with a view to making them more comfortable, while retaining something of the rustic elegance of the original buildings. This often involves the reverse of the restoration process described above. For example, the original thatch may be covered or replaced with a metal roof that preserves the shape and slope of the original roof but is easier and less expensive to maintain. Since traditional farmhouses are notoriously cold and drafty, other popular modifications include the addition

of ceilings and the installation of sealed windows. A traditional kitchen with its dirt floors and woodburning stoves may be remodeled, and though *tatami* mats, cushions, and low tables are retained in some rooms, other rooms are usually equipped with tables and chairs. When modern appliances and furniture are chosen with care, they can blend surprisingly well with the rustic but simple interior of a traditional farmhouse.

Above: An elegantly restored farmhouse featuring an open hearth (*irori*). In the adjacent room can be seen a traditional chest of drawers (*tansu*). Opening the sliding doors creates a spacious interior.

Kurashiki: A Rice Merchant Town

Kurashiki prospered in the Edo Period under the direct control of the Tokugawa shogunate. Built on the banks of canals, the town teemed with boats and barges loaded with rice and cotton destined for Osaka. This local produce was collected from nearby villages and stored in whitewashed, black-tiled *kura*, many of which have since been converted into museums, shops, teahouses, and inns.

Edo Period

Edo Period taxes were paid to the shogun in the form of rice. In the late sixteenth century, Ukita Hideie, lord of Okayama Castle, re-claimed tideland on the Inland Sea in western Honshu and established Kurashiki as the main rice-collecting depot for western Japan. Kura-shiki prospered not only as a collection depot for regional products but as an important wholesale and retail center where wealthy farmers engaged in making and selling *saké*, indigo, and other products. The city's name (*kura* means "storehouse") reflects this past emphasis upon mercantile activities.

Edo Period structures in Kurashiki consist primarily of thick-walled *kura* attached to businessmen's houses (*machiya*) that also were built in a matching *kura* style. Both *kura* and *machiya* had whitewashed walls, some of which were decorated with square tiles in vary-ing degrees of black and gray. Roofs were covered with black *hongawara buki* tiles.

During the Edo Period, the Kurashiki mag-istrate did not allow average citizens to build two-story *machiya*. As a consequence, rich merchants constructed houses that appeared to have two stories. In reality, the front area of the house consisted of a high open space with slat-covered windows on the upper part of the walls to let in light. In many cases, the back area of the house had a second floor that could be used for storage but could not be divided into rooms for living purposes. These basic principles of residential architecture are exemplified in what were formerly the houses of the Ōhara and Ōhashi families. Both houses have survived to the present time with relative-ly little alteration.

Built in 1795, the main building of the Ōhara family is 7 bays wide and 6.5 bays deep. It has a gabled roof covered with black tiles. Short extensions with their own roofs (*hisashi*) are attached to the gable ends. The wall of the main floor on the side facing the street is surfaced with square tiles. Built about the same time as the Ōhara house, the Ōhashi house has a samurai style gate (*nagayamon*), indicating the family's special status as descen-dants of a warrior family that served Toyotomi Hideyoshi. The Ōhashi residence is a typical *machiya* style house with several *tatami* rooms on one side of an earthen passage that runs from the front entrance to a door at the back. There are two six-mat rooms at the front that served as shops where the manager or his assistants met with customers. Larger *tatami* rooms in the interior of the house provided comfortable living space for the daily activities of the Ōhashi family.

Modern Period

With the demise of the Tokugawa shogunate at the time of the Meiji Restoration in 1868, Kurashiki lost its shogunal patronage, and its prosperity began to decline. Several promi-nent citizens and government officials decided to start a cotton spinning industry. With the backing of a wealthy local businessman, Ōhara Kōshirō, the Kurashiki Spinning Com-pany was constructed in 1888, using bricks imported from England in an attempt to re-create the spinning factory in Lancashire, the birth place of modern spinning. The fac-tory was a success and the president, Ōhara Magosaburō, used his wealth to collect famous Western paintings, which he housed in the Ōhara Museum of Art, constructed in 1930, the first Western art museum in Japan. His son established the well-known Kurashiki Museum of Folk Crafts and the Kurashiki Archaeology Museum, both in restored *kura*. Unlike most other *kura*, the warehouse in

Above: When cedar bough balls at a *saké* shop turn brown, customers know the new *saké* is ready.

Below: The former Ōhara house was built in typical Kurashiki style with white plaster and tiled walls.

Above left: Originally, stone-covered alleys facilitated the passage of carts carrying cotton. Today, most alleys have been resurfaced. Square tiles, a distinctive feature of the town, decorate the walls of the buildings flanking the alley.

Below left: The white plaster and tiles on the second floor of these shops provide a pleasant contrast to the dark wood of the ground floor.

Left: Two-story house built in the *kura* style, with white plaster, decorative tiles, and slatted windows (*Kurashiki-mado*), typical of the area. The house is located along one of Kurakishi's attractive willow-lined canals.

Below: Kurashikikan, the former town office, is a wooden pseudo-Western style building, which is now used as an information office.

which the Archaeology Museum is housed was originally a fish warehouse. It is the largest remaining *kura* in Kurashiki. The former factory of the Kurashiki Spinning Company, consisting of brick warehouses covered with ivy, was renovated as Kurashiki Ivy Square. Popular with tourists, it houses an award-winning hotel, museums, and shops.

Other buildings of interest include traditional inns such as the Ryokan Tsurugata, housed in the former Koyama residence. Constructed in 1744, it is the second oldest extant *machiya* in Kurashiki. Its main banquet room, originally a second-floor storage area, is 100 *tatami* mats in size. Another inn, Ryokan Kurashiki, is housed in the Meiji Period residence and *kura* of a former sugar merchant. Kurashikikan, the former town office, is a wooden two-story structure with a *sangawara buki* tile roof and horizontal board siding. Constructed in 1916, it is a good example of pseudo-Western style architecture, described later in the book.

Kurashiki escaped bombing during the war. As a result, it has been able to preserve many notable buildings from different historical periods making it a living outdoor museum of past architectural styles. Every year, millions of tourists visit Kurashiki to stroll along its canals and view its fascinating buildings, many of which are remodeled storehouses.

The Important Role of Storehouses

Above: Elevated storehouse from Amami-Oshima Island, originally found all over Japan, designed to protect grain from humidity and mice.

Above: Free-standing *kura* at Nishi Honganji Temple in Kyoto, which has a revolving vault in the center containing Buddhist texts.

Japanese storehouses have received little attention despite their important role in the development of Japanese culture and architecture. Prehistoric raised *kura* developed into early Shinto shrines and chiefs' dwellings, and ultimately were a major influence upon palace and residential architecture. *Kura* also evolved into forms as diverse as commercial warehouses, breweries, and the treasure houses of shrines and temples.

Early Developments

Some of the earliest government institutions of the Yamato State were the Sacred Storehouse where sacred objects were kept, the Great Storehouse that housed State possessions, including rice collected as taxes, and the Inner Storehouse for safeguarding the emperor's private possessions. Until recently, the Ministry of Finance was known as the Department of the Great Storehouse. These early government storehouses were probably raised off the ground like the prehistoric storehouses of the Jōmon, Yayoi, and Kofun Periods. In 701, a new legal code designated the Great Storehouse as one of the eight divisions of a bureaucracy modeled after Tang China. In the Heian Period, this government division, known as the Treasury, consisted of a block of office buildings and eight blocks of storehouses, located on the grounds of the Imperial Palace at Heiankyō.

The *shōsō* type *kura* (true storehouse), where valuables were kept, was distinguished from the *shakusō* (temporary storehouse). Because of its connection with things of value, the raised *shōsō kura* was especially prestigious and provided the prototype for Shinto shrines, chiefs' houses, and palaces. With the coming of Buddhism in the sixth century, temples constructed storehouses for safeguarding treasures such as the sutras. Buddhist storehouses were of two types: one (*azekura*) was a traditional raised floor structure with log cabin walls constructed of triangular shaped timbers that swelled in the rainy season to prevent moisture from entering and contracted in the cool, dry months to allow the circulation of air. The roof was covered either with tiles or cypress bark. The other was a post-and-beam structure with heavy wooden walls erected on the ground. The former style is exemplified by Shōsōin, the imperial repository from the Nara Period that still stands on the precincts of Tōdaiji Temple. Other *azekura* storehouses from this period can be found on the grounds of Tōshōdaiji Temple in Nara. A good example of the ground-level type of *kura* is the Old Sutra Storehouse of Kasuga Shrine in Nara, dating from the thirteenth century.

Later Developments

When Zen Buddhism was brought to Japan in the Kamakura Period, it introduced an octagonal-shaped sutra storehouse that had a revolving book cabinet in the center – a style that was later adopted by other denominations. By the Edo Period, it was commonly believed that turning the bookcase around once earned one as much religious merit as actually reading the scriptures. Over the years, most Shinto shrines, Buddhist temples, and houses of samurai and wealthy businessmen accumulated collections of paintings, calligraphy, and other arts and crafts that were stored in "treasure houses" that functioned as museums. Today, traditional treasure houses are being replaced with concrete structures better able to withstand wind and fire.

In the Kamakura Period, commercial warehouses were developed to store trade goods. Sometimes space in these better constructed warehouses was rented to others for the safekeeping of important documents and valuable objects such as jewels and metal coins. Thus, they functioned as an early type of bank. Eventually, commercial warehouses became commonplace in port cities, post towns, and castle towns, where the stable temperature and humidity provided by the thick walls made them suitable for making and storing fermented products such as *miso* paste and soy sauce.

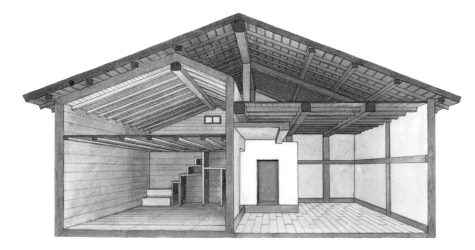

Kura were also useful for storing items such as art objects, *tatami* mats, and bedding materials used in villas, mansions, and early modern residences. Items were moved between residence and *kura*, depending upon the season and the occasion. In Japan's emerging towns and cities, raised storehouses were eventually abandoned in favor of ground-level post-and-beam structures erected on a foundation of heavy timbers. Lattices composed of strips of bamboo or wood were used to fill the spaces between the posts. The lattices were then covered with a clay and straw mixture and plastered. Roofs were either tiled or covered with clay. In the latter case, a secondary wood-en roof was constructed on top to protect the clay roof from rain. In the event of fire, the top roof could burn without affecting the secondary roof. Floors were equipped with slatted panels to allow air to enter and circulate to upper stories.

In areas with few earthquakes, *kura* walls were sometimes constructed of clay bricks or stones. The roof was made of wood, covered with tiles, and plastered on the underside. Alternatively, the structure was sometimes made of wood, around which stones were stacked. In some cases, the roof was covered with rocks fashioned into tile shapes to provide weight and protection from fire.

The Mausoleums at Nikkō

In accordance with a request made by Tokugawa Ieyasu, his mortuary tablet was enshrined a year after his death on Mount Nikkō, where he became guardian of the Kanto area. The original buildings at Nikkō were simple, but they were redone much more elaborately a few years later by Ieyasu's grandson Iemitsu, who wished to demonstrate the wealth and power of the Tokugawa shogunate.

History

Mount Nikkō has long been a holy spot. In 766, a Buddhist priest, Shōdō-shōnin, built a hermitage on top of the mountain. Over the years, additional temples were added by famous persons such as Kōbō Daishi, founder of Shingon Buddhism, and various lords of the Genji clan, including Yoritomo, the first shogun. During the Kamakura Period, a member of the imperial family was appointed abbot of the complex, a tradition that continued through the Edo Period.

When the first Tokugawa shogun, Ieyasu, died in 1616, his ashes were interred in Kunōsan Temple in Shizuoka Prefecture. The following year, Jigen Daishi, 53rd abbot of the Nikkō temples, and friend of Ieyasu, moved the ashes to the newly constructed Tōshōgū Shrine in a heavily forested area on

Mount Nikkō, and Ieyasu was enshrined as a *gongen* – a syncretic deity that is both a *kami* and an avatar (incarnation of the Buddha). The original buildings, constructed in the simple Wayō (Japanese) style, were dismantled 20 years later by Ieyasu's grandson Iemitsu, and the shrine was rebuilt in the more elaborate Chinese Zen style. Most of the buildings are covered inside and out with gold leaf and black and red lacquer, and are decorated with brightly painted carvings of flowers, mythical birds and animals, and human figures.

After the death of Iemitsu in 1651, the emperor granted him the posthumous Buddhist name of Taiyūin, and in 1653 the Taiyūin Mausoleum for Iemitsu's ashes was constructed near his grandfather's mausoleum. Set in a dense forest of cryptomeria trees, the Taiyūin Mausoleum is just as ornate as the Tōshōgū. It is, however, smaller and considered by most to be more elegant and aesthetically balanced. Like the Tōshōgū, the path to the main buildings is marked by a series of three gates and subsidiary buildings such as storehouses. The main buildings – the Honden, Ainoma, and Haiden – are mostly in the Chinese Zen style and are connected to each other with covered corridors. The buildings are covered inside and out with gold leaf and black and red lacquer, and are decorated with brightly painted carvings of flowers and Chinese dragons.

World Heritage Site

In 1999, both mausoleums, together with other nearby buildings, such as Futarasan Shrine, the oldest extant building in the area, were registered as a World Heritage Site. The complex consists of 103 buildings, of which nine are classified as National Treasures and 94 as Important Cultural Properties. The rationale for selecting Nikkō as a World Heritage Site was, first, that most of the

buildings are the work of some of Japan's greatest seventeenth-century artists; secondly, the buildings are among the finest examples of the Gongen style which exercised a major influence on subsequent mausoleum and shrine architecture, and thirdly, the site played a crucial political role, as it was regularly visited by envoys from the imperial court in Kyoto, successive shoguns, as well as diplomats from Korea. This rationale acknowledges the fact that Iemitsu was successful in achieving his goal of making Nikkō a showpiece of Tokugawa power.

Reconstruction of the Tōshōgū

The Tōshōgū and Taiyūin mausoleums are the most ornate and expensive buildings in Japan. When Tōshōgū Shrine was rebuilt, Iemitsu drew roughly 55,000 million yen from the private inheritance left by his grandfather Ieyasu, to hire more than 15,000 laborers and some of Japan's finest artists and craftsmen, who contributed more than 4.8 million man days on the project. Construction work was begun in November 1634, under the direction of Kōra Munehiro, who had been involved in the building of Ieyasu's detached house in Fushimi, Kyoto, as well as Katsura Rikyū Detached Palace in Kyoto. Total construction cost was roughly equal to the national annual budget at the time for the whole of Japan. Such a large-scale project, which would have been impossible in earlier periods, benefited from advances that had recently been made in architectural techniques such as elevation plans, as well as from a system for obtaining estimates, bids, and contractors.

The site flows up the slope via stone stairways that connect many different kinds of buildings as one passes through the Omotemon (front gate), Yōmeimon Gate, Karamon Gate, and on to the Main Shrine. Color coordination was under the direction of Kanō Tanyū, the most noted artist of the Edo Period.

The reconstruction of Tōshōgū was also influenced by developments in the decorative tradition. Following the introduction of Buddhism, many Shinto shrines began to use vermilion colored lacquer on their exteriors, in the fashion of Buddhist temples. Interiors, however, were generally left simple. By the end of the Muromachi Period, the use of color had become more prominent in shrines than in Buddhist temples. The following Momoyama and Edo Periods saw the increased use of brightly painted three-dimensional sculp-

tures. This decorative trend reached its culmination in Nikkō Tōshōgū, where both exterior and interior surfaces were covered with colorful carved, gilded, painted, and lacquered figures and designs that can best be described as baroque.

The reconstruction of Tōshōgū took a year and a half to complete. Ieyasu's spirit was then moved to the shrine in a grand ceremony held in April 1636. Although the extravagance at Nikkō is scorned by many for its lack of taste, the craftsmanship has to be admired for its sheer skill.

Above: Constructed in 1619 by the second Tokugawa shogun, Hidetada, the main building of Futarasan Shrine is the oldest extant building at Nikkō.

Below: Simplified layout of part of the Nikkō grounds.

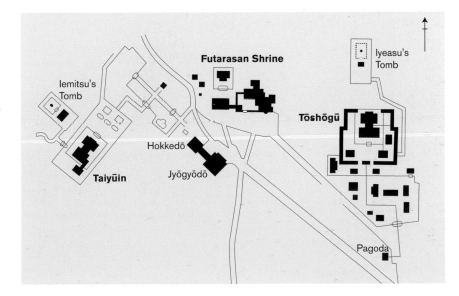

Tōshōgū Shrine at Nikkō

The buildings of Tōshōgū were arranged without excessive regard to symmetry. The site flows up the slope via stone stairways. Along the way, many different kinds of buildings are encountered as one passes through the Omotemon (front gate), Yōmeimon Gate, Karamon Gate, and on to the Main Shrine. The overall plan, which is extremely complex, was designed to create a particular psychological effect. For example, the Yōmeimon Gate is characterized by a profusion of colors that would be startling were it not for the fact that all of the colors are used, in a more sparing fashion, in the buildings leading up to the gate. To this explosion of color in the Yōmeimon Gate is added an abundance of white, suggesting that one is about to enter sacred space. This ingenious color scheme was produced by Kanō Tanyū, Japan's most famous painter in the early part of the Edo Period.

Some of the best-known buildings in the complex are three sacred storehouses, sacred stables decorated with the famous carvings of the "hear, speak and see no evil monkeys," a revolving library containing 7,000 sutras, bell and drum towers, the Haiden (Oratory Hall), and the Honden (Main Hall). Past the main buildings, a flight of stone steps leads up to Ieyasu's tomb.

The contrast between the aesthetic restraint of the Grand Shrines at Ise and the ornate splendor of the Tokugawa mausoleums at Nikkō could hardly be more pronounced. Yet both are majestic in their own ways. They are monuments to the dynamism of Japanese culture with its dual emphasis upon both restraint and exuberance, depending upon the circumstances and patrons.

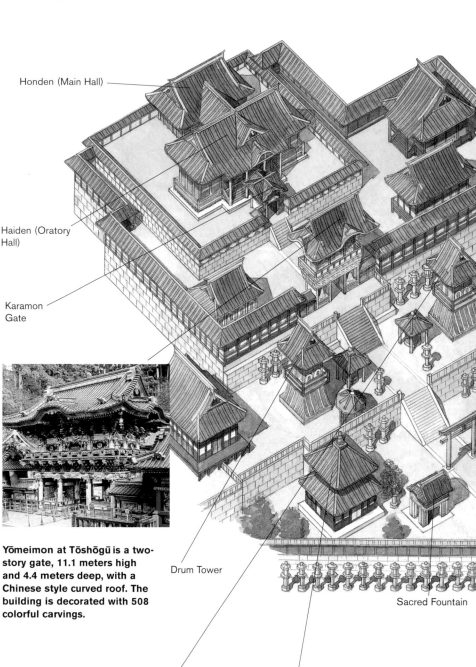

Honden (Main Hall)

Haiden (Oratory Hall)

Karamon Gate

Drum Tower

Sacred Fountain

Yōmeimon at Tōshōgū is a two-story gate, 11.1 meters high and 4.4 meters deep, with a Chinese style curved roof. The building is decorated with 508 colorful carvings.

Detail from the Bell Tower, showing the elaborate bracketing system and colored decorations.

One of three sacred storehouses, this building is a repository for implements used in the Spring and Autumn Festivals.

Detail of the Omotemon Gate, the first entrance to Tōshōgū, which houses four meter-tall statues of fierce guardian deities on both sides.

Five-story Pagoda

Entrance Gate (*Torii*)

The famous "hear no evil, speak no evil, and see no evil" monkeys, derived from the three main principles of Tendai Buddhism, carved on the lintel of the Sacred Stable at Tōshōgū.

Left: The library houses an octagonal revolving book stack containing a complete collection of scriptures.

Sukiya Style Villas and Palaces

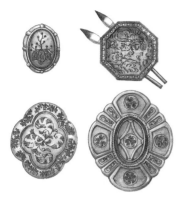

Above: *Hikite* are metal plates with depressed centers used for pushing and pulling sliding doors. Often enameled, they provide beautiful examples of Japanese metal craftsmanship.

Below: The present Imperial Palace in Tokyo, built in 1968 on the grounds of the original Edo Castle, is in the Katsura Rikyū tradition, with straight lines and elegant simplicity. Drawing after a photograph provided by the Imperial Household Agency, Tokyo.

The Sukiya style is an informal version of Shoin architecture. Whereas Shoin buildings aimed at formality through the use of ornately decorated walls, heavy squared timbers, and decorated ceilings, the Sukiya style, which borrowed many of its techniques from the teahouse, emphasized the use of natural materials, such as poles with the bark left on them, to create a relaxed atmosphere. Another difference is that the roof eaves of Shoin style buildings have a slight upward curve in the tradition of shrines and temples, whereas Sukiya style buildings have a slight downward curve.

Sukiya Aesthetic Taste

Shoin architecture, which developed out of the Shinden style in the Muromachi Period, continued to be used in later periods in buildings designed for formal occasions. But the atmosphere of Shoin architecture was too grand for the daily activities of the upper classes. Consequently, the Shoin style was modified for daily life by using more delicate structural members and attempting to create a more rustic atmosphere, dictated by the canons of aesthetic restraint and understatement associated with the tea ceremony. At the same time, the general proportions and elegance of the Shoin style were retained. The result was a masterful creation that many believe to represent the essence of Japanese traditional architecture.

The influential German architect Bruno Taut proclaimed that the two high points of Japanese architecture are Ise Jingū and the Sukiya style detached palace, Katsura Rikyū. This claim highlights the fact that Ise Jingū, with its simple elegance and preference for natural materials, provided the prototype for Japanese residential architecture, including palaces, villas, and early modern residential architecture. When the aesthetic principles expressed at Ise were combined with the aesthetic principles developed in the Way of Tea, the result was a level of taste so refined and highly sophisticated that it represents one of the major contributions of Japanese culture to the world.

Seisonkaku Villa

Situated at one end of Kanazawa's famous Kenrokuen Garden, Seisonkaku Villa was created in 1863 by Maeda Nariyasu, the thirteenth Lord of the Kaga clan, as a gift for his mother. Seisonkaku is a shingled mansion about 1000 square meters in size. The Hiku-ku-tei (Garden of the Flying Crane) is one of Seisonkaku's three gardens. It has the tranquil atmosphere of a tea garden with rocks, moss, and a quiet stream that loops through the veranda of the villa. This allows the stream to be viewed even in the winter when shutters close the veranda off from the snow.

The downstairs rooms of the villa are all finished in the formal Shoin style (described

earlier), while the more colorful upstairs rooms are in the Sukiya style. The upstairs consists of seven rooms with elaborate ceilings and walls. Each room is named for the material used or for the style of the ceiling. The Gunjō-no-ma (Ultramarine Chamber) has blue cornices and panel board joints in the coved, coffered ceiling. The adjacent Gunjō-shoken-no-ma is a small reading room with a blue

ceiling, purple walls, and a black *tokonoma* (alcove) with a raised floor. To one side of the alcove are staggered shelves which share pillars with the alcove, a unique design feature that is both elegant and space-saving. In front of the alcove is an elevated mat where one can sit at the built-in desk (*shoin*). The Adjiro-no-ma has a ceiling made of split cedar wickerwork (*ajiro*). All three rooms feature *shoji* windows

Above: Rinshunkaku Villa in Sankeien Garden, Yokohama, is a relocated Edo Period *daimyō* mansion. It is an outstanding example of Sukiya style architecture, with interior panels painted by Kanō school artists.

Left: The restored 100-year-old Nakamura house (see page 13) has two adjoining *tatami* rooms once used as reception rooms where lacquerware producers exchanged information on their trade. The black lacquered wicker boxes were used as portable trunks for their products.

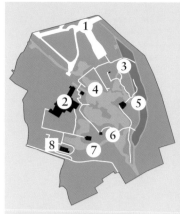

Above: Simplified layout of Katsura Rikyū Detached Palace. The staggered buildings of the palace are situated to the west of a large pond that forms the nucleus of a stroll garden containing islands, bridges, rocks, and trees. Three teahouses and a private temple are scattered around the grounds.

1 Omotemon (front gate)
2 Shoin buildings (palace)
3 Machiai (waiting area for
  a tea ceremony)
4 Geppa-rō Teahouse
5 Shōkin-tei Teahouse
6 Shōka-tei Teahouse
7 Onrin-dō Memorial Chapel
8 Shōi-ken Teahouse

Above right: The buildings of Katsura Rikyū Detached Palace are raised on posts in the Ise Jingū and palace tradition.

Right: Ichi-no-ma in the Shin-goten of Katsura Rikyū. The exterior sliding doors, covered with translucent rice paper (shōji), can be opened to provide views of the garden. Both photographs courtesy of the Imperial Household Agency, Kyoto.

Katsura Rikyū Detached Palace

The most famous example of Sukiya style architecture is Katsura Rikyū, built around 1615 by Prince Hachijō-no-miya Toshihito, the younger brother of Emperor Goyōzei. Prince Hachijō-no-miya received the Katsura estate from the second Tokugawa shogun, Hidetada, in return for his services as a liaison between the imperial family and the Tokugawa shogunate. Originally, the estate was the site of Fujiwara-no-Michinaga's Heian Period mansion, which may have provided the setting for some of the episodes in Lady Murasaki Shikibu's famous novel, *Genji Monogatari* (The Tale of Genji). The original mansion was no longer extant when Katsura Rikyū was constructed by Prince Hachijō-no-miya in the early 1600s. More buildings were added in 1641 and 1662, resulting in the asymmetrical layout of the complex today, composed of four connected structures: the Old Shoin (Ko-shoin), the Middle Shoin (Chū-shoin), the Music Room (Gakki-no-ma), and the New Palace (Shin-goten).

The buildings of Katsura Rikyū Detached Palace are raised on posts, in the Ise Shrine and palace tradition. The spaces under the buildings are enclosed with white plastered walls, interspersed with bamboo laths. This raised style of architecture facilitates air circulation and enhances the view of the stroll garden, consisting of artificial hills, ponds, and streams on a property of some 56,000 square meters. The garden, which is connected to the palace by paths that wander through an ever-changing miniature landscape, was designed to form an integral whole with the buildings.

The palace buildings, located west of the pond area, have hipped-and-gable roofs, shingled with cypress bark. The staggered arrangement of the four buildings is described as "geese in flight" – a formation that maximizes fresh air and views of the garden. The floors and eaves of each building are on slightly different levels, achieving what is referred to as a "cascade effect." The floors of the palace are covered with *tatami* mats, and the interior space is divided by tastefully decorated sliding paper doors (*fusuma*). Spaces between the exterior posts can be opened and closed with sliding doors made of wooden frames covered with translucent rice paper (*shōji*) that admit light.

One of the rooms in the Old Shoin, the Irori-no-ma (Room of the Hearth), has a sunken fire pit. To prevent fire, all of the doors are made of wooden board instead of the usual paper. Other rooms in the Ko-shoin were used for receiving guests, as well as for guest bedrooms. Attached to the main room of the Old Shoin is a Moon Viewing Platform facing the pond, where frequent parties were held to view the full moon, write Chinese and Japanese poetry, and indulge in gastronomic delights. The elevated platform has no walls or roof. Its floor is made of thin bamboo stems that provide a feeling of informality.

The Middle Shoin is smaller than the Old Shoin, but it was built in a more formal Shoin style. The emperor's seat was located in a room called Ichi-no-ma (No. 1 room). The room has only six *tatami* mats, but a large alcove with landscape paintings on its walls provides a sense of space. The Ichi-no-ma is connected to the Music Room by a veranda.

The Music Room has an alcove where a *koto* (Japanese harp) was placed and a small window that looks out into the inner court. Attached to the Music Room is a veranda with a railing and a recessed bench where occupants could sit to watch sports, such as Japanese style football, archery, and horse racing being played on the large lawn, shown above.

with glass panes imported from the Netherlands. The glass permitted occupants to engage in winter snow viewing without opening the sliding doors. A fourth room, the Etchū-no-ma, has a ceiling made of cedar boards from a town in Etchū, currently called Toyama.

Rinshunkaku Villa

Sankeien Garden in Honmoku, Yokohama City, established in 1906 by HaraTomitarō, a wealthy Yokohama silk merchant better known by his pseudonym, Hara Sankei, is an 18 hectare park whose trees, flowers, and ponds form a beautiful setting for the former Hara family mansion, Kakushōkaku ("crane-flying pavilion"), as well as a number of historic buildings which he collected and relocated from Kyoto and Nara, including Rinshunkaku, an Edo Period warrior mansion.

Rinshunkaku was originally built in 1649 along the Kino River in Wakayama as a summer villa for the first Lord of Kishu Province, Tokugawa Yorinobu. Hara Sankei acquired it in 1906, restored it at his garden in 1917, and renamed it Rinshunkaku, literally "the spring-viewing pavilion." It is one of the few remaining villas from the feudal period and is an outstanding example of Sukiya style architecture. It has three wings. The first has antechambers for guests and vassals; the second has chambers where the lord would meet guests; the third served mainly as living rooms for the consort. The first wing is notable for the paintings on the *fusuma* sliding doors done by leading artists of the time, including two Kanō school artists, Tanyū and Yasunobu.

Other structures in the garden which were relocated include a 1457 three-storied pagoda from Tōmyōji Temple in Kyoto, old temple structures and buildings from Hidyoshi's Fushimi Monoyama and Nijō castles, and an old thatched house from Gifu Prefecture.

Other Sukiya Style Examples

Manshuin, a Kyoto temple belonging to the Tendai sect, traditionally was headed by an abbot selected from the imperial family. This kind of temple, where royalty lived, is known as *monzeki*. Manushin has two Shoin style buildings, the Greater Shoin and the Lesser Shoin. The Lesser Shoin, done in the Sukiya style, consists of two main rooms, the Twilight Room and the Mount Fuji Room, plus two tearooms and a kitchen. Although the two main rooms contain the basic features of the Shoin style, such as a *jōdan* (raised area for receiving guests or retainers), decorative alcove, shelves, and built-in desk, these features are arranged in a non-traditional style, reflecting the personality and taste of the designer. This emphasis upon uniqueness and personal idiosyncrasies is one of the defining characteristics of the more individualistic Sukiya style.

Built a year after the construction of Manshuin, the Kuro Shoin room of Nishi Honganji Temple in Kyoto, is another good example of early Shoin style architecture. The Kuro Shoin was designed as an intimate area, composed of several adjacent rooms, where the abbot of the temple could conduct personal interviews and relax from his official duties. In keeping with this purpose, the Kuro Shoin, meaning "Black Shoin," received its name from the fact that the pillars and ceiling were darkened with black lacquer. The rooms are decorated with ink landscape paintings and natural woods that create an exquisite but subtle atmosphere, in contrast to the magnificent formality of the main audience hall and the Shiro Shon (White Shoin) at the same temple. The best known room in the complex, Ichi no Ma (First Room), includes standard Shoin features such as a decorative alcove and built-in desk, but they are arranged in a way that departs from the formal Shoin style.

The Lesser Shoin of Manshuin and the Kuro Shoin of Nishi Honganji Temple have many similarities, which are not accidental. Manshuin was built in 1656 by Ryōshō, the younger brother of Prince Toshihito, whose daughter was the wife of the abbot at Nishi Honganji Temple.

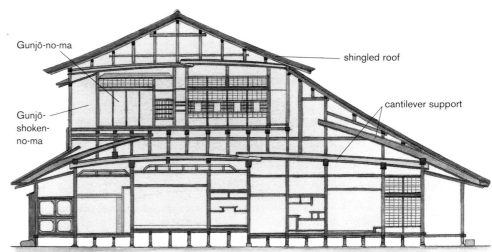

Gunjō-no-ma

Gunjō-shoken-no-ma

shingled roof

cantilever support

Above: Cross-section of Seison-kaku Villa with Shoin style rooms on the first floor and Sukiya style rooms on the top floor. The building is one of the most elegant of the few remaining samurai mansions in Japan. Drawing after Seisonkaku brochure.

Below: The Gungō-shoken-no-ma, a small Sukiya style reading room in Seisonkaku Villa, known for its unusual colors.

Above: The guest room in Yōshida Sansō, an expansive two-story imperial villa built in Kyoto in the 1930s, currently an exclusive inn. The subdued colors and natural wood convey the exquisite tranquility associated with Sukiya style architecture.

Opposite: The beautifully paneled doors at the main entrance (*genkan*) to Yōshida Sansō are derived from Art Deco motifs. The sliding doors divide the *genkan* from the interior of the villa.

A Modern Adaptation

Yōshida Sansō, currently an exclusive inn in Kyoto, was constructed in 1932 in the foothills of Kyoto's Mount Yoshida as a private residence for Higashi Fushiminomiya, uncle of the current Japanese emperor, Akihito. Higashi Fushiminomiya lived at Yōshida Sansō while attending Kyoto University.

In the spirit of greater freedom promoted by the Sukiya style of architecture, the villa combines traditional Shoin style features, such as *tatami* mats, a recessed alcove, and staggered shelves, with modern touches inspired by the Art Deco movement, which was

popular in Japan in the early Showa Period.

The villa is constructed entirely of *hinoki* (Japanese cypress), the pieces of which are joined in a traditional manner without the use of nails. Each frontal roof tile and *fusuma* (sliding door) handle bears the design of the imperial chrysanthemum, a design element restricted to buildings associated with imperial patronage.

Yōshida Sansō was designed by one of Japan's master builders, Nishioka Tsunekazu, who also supervised restoration work at some of Nara's most famous Buddhist temples, such as Hōryūji and Yakushiji.

Theaters and Sumo Rings

The Edo Period was a time of relative stability, peace, and prosperity. The arts and crafts flourished and culture spread throughout Japanese society. Traditional forms of entertainment, such as the Noh drama, continued to appeal to the aristocratic classes, but new forms of entertainment, such as Kabuki, Bunraku, and Sumo developed to meet the needs of ordinary people.

Noh

Noh theater has its roots in Heian Period Sarugaku ("monkey music") which combined several earlier forms of popular entertainment. Sarugaku gradually developed into more sophisticated plays used by shrines and temples to explain religious concepts to the common people. Kannami, a Shinto priest at Kasuga Shrine in Nara, and his son Zeami gave Sarugaku a more artistic form, which attracted the attention of the Ashikaga shogun Yoshimitsu. Under his patronage, as well as the influence of Zen Buddhism, Kannami and Zeami developed Noh theater, which combines acting, a chorus, and an orchestra to produce a graceful and mysterious art form that some have compared to ancient Greek theater. The dominant aesthetic idea is *yūgen*, a deep level of beauty that can only be suggested by subtle nuances of sound and movement. If the repertoire contains more than one drama, plays may be separated by fast-moving comedies known as Kyōgen, sometimes performed independently.

In the beginning, Noh theater was performed on existing stages of shrines or temples, or else employed temporary stages constructed for each occasion. Noh became popular among the ruling classes, with the result that many *daimyo* had Noh stages built in their private residences. Despite its humble origins, Noh theater was too sophisticated for the average person to understand and never developed the popular appeal of Kabuki and Bunraku, described below. Nevertheless, Noh attracted a following among educated commoners in the Feudal Period. Today, Noh drama is normally performed in a permanent theater containing a stage with its own roof, as well as seats for the audience. Before the play begins, the musicians and members of the chorus enter to sit at the rear and side of the main stage. Actors, some of whom are masked, enter the main stage via a causeway. Stage props are kept to a bare minimum.

Bunraku

In the early seventeenth century, *jōruri* (the recitation of traditional tales) was combined with musical accompaniment by the *shamisen* (a three-stringed instrument) and the folk puppet theater of the island of Awaji – an amalgamation that came to be known as *ningyō jōruri* (telling a story with puppets). Eventually, the new dramatic form was called Bunraku, based upon the first syllable of the name of Bunzaemon, an entrepreneur who

Below: Noh stage at the Nara Prefectural Public Hall. A causeway for the entry and exit of actors connects with the main stage, a 17-square meter structure made of cypress wood, whose only decoration is a large pine tree painted on the backboard. In front of the causeway and main stage is a bed of white gravel and three small pine trees, symbolizing the fact that 0originally Noh stages were outdoors, often on the grounds of shrines and temples. Today, the audience sits in air-conditioned comfort, protected from insects, noise, and weather.

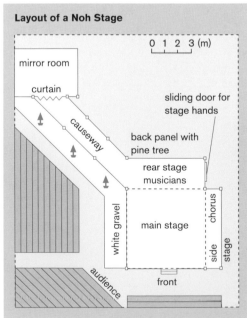

Layout of a Noh Stage

mirror room

curtain

causeway

sliding door for stage hands

back panel with pine tree

rear stage musicians

white gravel

main stage

side stage

chorus

0 1 2 3 (m)

audience

front

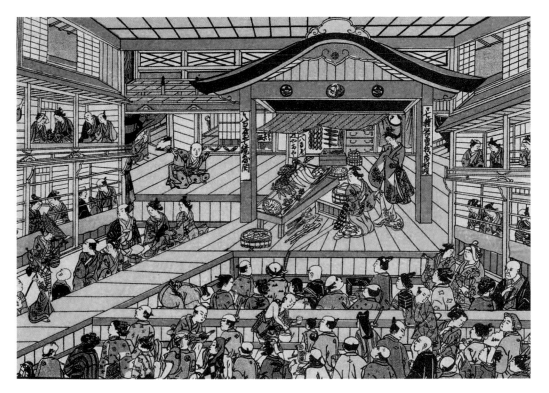

Left: Woodblock print by Oku-mura Masanobu of a Kabuki theater in the Edo Period (around 1740). The pitched roof over the main stage is reminiscent of the Noh stage on which Kabuki began. The posts and pitched roof were eventually abandoned as they blocked the audience's view. Seats extended to the sides of the main stage, and sometimes balconies were added behind the stage. If seating was still insufficient, the patrons were allowed to sit on the stage surrounding the actors. Demeanor, particularly in the private boxes, tended to be lax, resulting in the enactment of regulations for the purpose of improving "public morality" and ensuring a greater semblance of order.

took a troupe of performers from Awaji Island to Osaka, where it became popular. In 1984, a national Bunraku theater was established in Osaka. The theater is a modern five-story steel and concrete building containing the main auditorium as well as a rehearsal hall, training rooms, lecture rooms, conference rooms, administrative offices, and restaurants. This beautiful edifice has enhanced the popularity of Bunraku today.

Bunraku puppets are manipulated by two or three puppeteers. The main puppeteer, who is unmasked, operates the head and right hand of the puppet, while the other limbs are moved by masked assistants.

Kabuki

Kabuki is a form of theater in which actors with painted faces and extravagant costumes perform traditional stories to the accompaniment of chanting and *shamisen* music. Actions are exaggerated and stage sets are frequently changed, to provide a lively form of entertainment with broad appeal. Kabuki plays are about historical events, moral conflicts in love relationships, and the like. Originally, Kabuki entertainment was the domain of women who also provided after-hours recreation of a more intimate sort. Eventually, government regulations led to a more formal and profes-

sional form of entertainment in which all roles were played by men. Some male Kabuki actors specialized in playing female roles (*onnagata*).

In 1652, the shogun decreed that Kabuki performances be based upon the dialogue, acting techniques, and realism of Kyōgen – fast-moving comedies that are performed between Noh plays. Although the style of

Below: The Bunraku stage is specially constructed to accommodate three-person puppets. The puppeteers operate behind a solid railing attached to the front of the stage to conceal the lower part of their bodies. There is a raised platform called a *yuka* on one or both sides of the main stage for the *shamisen* players and chanters (one or more of each) who provide music and narrate the story of the play.

Above: Kureha-za, a popular local theater constructed in the 1870s in the present Ikeda City, Osaka Prefecture, has broad eaves and a drummer's balcony on the gabled wall. In addition to Kabuki plays, modern dramas and political plays were performed at this theater. In 1971, the theater was moved to the Meiji Mura Museum near Nagoya.

Right: Minami-za, a modern Kabuki theater in Kyoto, constructed on the site where Kabuki was born. The descendent of a small Edo Period playhouse, Minami-za is the oldest working theater in Japan. The baroque style seen here is often used in contemporary Kabuki theaters. The pitched roof seen on the interior of the woodblock print described above has been moved to the exterior of Minami-za.

acting became more highly formalized, Kabuki became easier for the common people to understand since it employed the spoken language of the day, thereby increasing its popularity.

At first Kabuki was performed on a Noh stage, but in the seventeenth century, Kabuki adopted a larger stage, a curtain (which made it easier to change sets), and the *hanamichi* (causeway leading from the actors' room to the stage). Stage left (*kamite*), just outside the arena of action, is regarded as the place of honor, occupied by high-ranking guests, and important officials. The trap door (*suppon*) located on the *hanamichi* is used for the entrance and exit of ghosts and other superhuman characters. An unusual feature of the Kabuki stage is a circular platform (*mawaributai*) that can be rotated to allow a new scene to begin just as the old scene is being completed.

Many of the best-loved stories for Kabuki theater were written in the late seventeenth century by the famous Chikamatsu Monzaemon, who drew on some of the same traditional stories used in the Noh theater. Chikamatsu eventually abandoned Kabuki in order to write plays for Bunraku, which, for a time, became so popular that Kabuki actors had to imitate puppets to attract an audience. By the middle of the eighteenth century, however, when the revolving stage was added to the Kabuki theater, Kabuki surpassed Bunraku in popularity. It continues to attract a full house today.

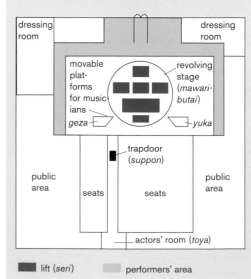

Layout of a Kabuki Stage

dressing room · dressing room

movable platforms for musicians · revolving stage (*mawaributai*)

geza · *yuka*

trapdoor (*suppon*)

public area · seats · seats · public area

actors' room (*toya*)

■ lift (*seri*)   ▨ performers' area

Sumo

Sumo is a Japanese style of wrestling and Japan's national sport. Dating back to the Tomb Mound Period, Sumo was used to entertain the deities and thereby ensure divine protection and a bountiful harvest. By the Nara Period, Sumo had become closely associated with the imperial court where it provided entertainment for the aristocratic classes. In the Edo Period, Sumo became a popular form of entertainment. Matches were often conducted on the grounds of Shinto shrines to help raise money for the repair of shrine buildings.

Much of the original Shinto symbolism can still be seen today. The match takes place in a ring (*dohyō*) – a raised platform about 5.4 meters in diameter. A new ring is made for each tournament from compressed clay covered with sand. Over the ring is a roof (*tsuriyane*) built in the style of a Shinto shrine roof. Both the ring and the roof are constructed inside a building large enough to house the audience. Originally, the roof was supported by four posts, but because of complaints that the posts blocked the view of the audience, eventually the roof was hung from the ceiling of the building in which it is enclosed, and the four posts were replaced by tassels, symbolizing the four seasons and the traditional Chinese deities associated with the four cardinal directions. Before fighting, Sumo wrestlers enact an ancient Shinto purification ritual by throwing salt into the ring and the bout is officiated by a referee dressed as a samurai from the Kamakura Period. The black court hat of gauze resembles the traditional headgear of a Shinto priest.

The goal of the match is to force the opponent out of the ring or to cause him to touch the ground with any part of his body other than his feet. The fights themselves usually last only a few seconds and in rare cases up to one minute or longer. Though Sumo wrestlers are generally very large and capable of applying a great deal of force, they are also expected to demonstrate considerable skill.

Sumo was designated as the national sport of Japan in 1909. Because of its emphasis on formality and tradition, Sumo is a unique martial art that has attracted much attention in other countries. Tournaments are held six times a year in Japan, rotating among Tokyo (three times), Osaka, Nagoya, and Fukuoka (one time each), and last for 15 days each time. Good attendance should help guarantee the survival of the traditional sport.

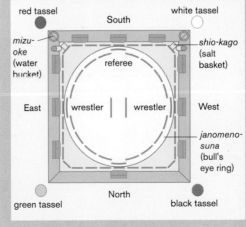

Above: A Sumo ring is covered with a Shinto style roof suspended by 22-mm-thick cables from the ceiling of the large stadium in which the ring is enclosed. The roof can be retracted when the stadium is used for other purposes. The Sumo ring itself is constructed anew for each tournament.

Left: Layout of a Sumo ring, showing the position of the wrestlers and referee before the match begins.

Japanese Architecture in Transition

The Meiji Restoration of 1868 is the dividing line between "traditional" and "modern" Japan. Early Modern Japan is the period between the Meiji Restoration and the end of World War II. During this period, Western culture had a significant influence upon public buildings, whereas architectural traditions associated with the daily life of the common people continued relatively unchanged.

Above: This square tower from a Western style post office, originally at Uji Yamada, was constructed in 1871. It has horizontal milled wood siding and a copper-covered dome.

Below: This Western style residence favored by the élite in the Meiji Period was constructed in Tokyo around 1880. It is now located at Meiji Mura.

Meiji Period (1868–1912)

Dissatisfaction with the Tokugawa government, combined with military pressure from the West, led to the Meiji Restoration of 1868, which abolished feudalism and returned power to the emperor. Following the defeat of the Tokugawa shogunate, Japan became a constitutional monarchy with a parliament. An ambitious program of modernization was fueled by the nationalistic ideology of State Shinto. The goal was to achieve economic and military modernization as quickly as possible to avoid colonization by the West. Young people were sent to Europe and the US to learn about banking, rail and road building, and to acquire the skills necessary for running a modern country. Model factories were established and subsidized, and many people in rural areas moved to the cities to work in the new factories. A mass program of indoctrination encouraged individuals of all ages and walks of life to sacrifice in the interests of building a nation that could overcome nearly three centuries of isolation and compete with the West.

Foreign advisers were brought to Japan and Western culture swept the country. It became fashionable to wear Western style clothing, eat Western food, and build Western style buildings. The newly established parliament, the Diet, even debated introducing English as the official language and importing Western women to refresh the gene pool. Instruction in traditional painting techniques was replaced in the schools by Western style oil painting and watercolors, many Buddhist monasteries were destroyed, and priceless Buddhist images were discarded or sold.

The modernization program was so successful that Japan embarked upon a series of international military adventures, defeating China in 1895 and Russia in 1905, followed by the annexation of the Ryūkyūs, southern Sakhalin, and Korea. Almost overnight, Japan had become a formidable world power.

Subsequent Periods

The Meiji Period ended with the death of the Meiji emperor. In the following Taisho Period (1912–26), the authoritarian measures of the Meiji oligarchy gave way to a democratic era characterized by true party government, increased involvement of people in politics, the growth of labor unions, and an economic boom fueled by World War I. An educated middle class provided support for the growth of radio, newspapers, magazines, and books. Eventually, Japan's new democracy lost ground to the rising power of an adventurist military.

In the following Showa Period (1926–89), the military took control and began a policy of military expansion that culminated in the Sino-Japanese War and World War II. After its defeat in World War II, Japan was occupied by a foreign power for the first time in its history. The occupying power was an Allied military force under the direction of an American, General Douglas MacArthur. Democracy was re-established and a new Constitution written. In return for cooperating with the occupation, Emperor Hirohito (posthumously named Emperor Showa) was allowed to remain on the Chrysanthemum Throne. The longest lived monarch in Japanese history, Emperor Hirohito died in 1989, ushering in the present Heisei Period under Emperor Akihito.

Western Influence on Architecture

The architecture of public buildings, primarily those associated with government and business, experienced significant transformation in the Meiji Period. New styles, techniques, and materials were adopted from the West, including the use of stone and brick, thereby paving the way for steel, concrete, and glass. Many Meiji buildings were destroyed by earthquakes, war, and unbridled postwar industrial growth. Fortunately, some of the best examples of Meiji Period architecture have been preserved at Meiji Mura (Meiji Village), which opened near Nagoya in 1965 as an open-air museum. Meiji Mura contains more than 60 buildings, originally destined for destruction, which were purchased and moved from various parts of Japan and elsewhere.

In an attempt to develop modern technology as rapidly as possible, the Meiji government hired experts, including engineers and architects from abroad. Following a disastrous fire in the Ginza-Tsukuji area of Tokyo in 1872, the government hired Thomas James Waters, a British engineer, to rebuild the area – the first example of modern urban planning in Japan. By 1877, the main thoroughfare of the Ginza was lined with European style brick buildings.

Another foreigner who had a major impact upon Japanese architecture was Josiah Condor (1852–1920), an Englishman, who arrived in Japan in 1877 at the age of 25 to serve as professor of architecture at the Imperial College of Engineering and consultant to the Ministry of Public Works. Between1878 and 1907, Condor designed over 50 major buildings in Tokyo, including the Tokyo Imperial Museum in Ueno, the largest brick building in Japan.

Although Japan soon began training its own architects and engineers, foreigners continued to come to Japan in subsequent periods. Two of the best known were the American architect Frank Lloyd Wright (1869–1959), who designed the Imperial Hotel in Tokyo, and the French architect Charles E. Jeanneret, better known as Le Corbusier (1887–1965), who designed the National Museum of Western Art in Tokyo.

Nomenclature

Following the prevalent Japanese custom of coining new words by combining and shortening two or more foreign words, the term "motra" (modern–traditional) will be used in the following pages to refer to traditional style buildings which were constructed in the modern period, that is, after 1868.

There are three types of motra. Type 1 motra are buildings whose basic structure and appearance are both traditional, such as residences, inns, shops, and neighborhood shrines that carried Edo Period styles into the modern era.

Type 2 motra are buildings whose basic structure is traditional but whose appearance is not, such as modern houses with synthetic siding and asphalt shingles that utilize traditional post-and-beam framing techniques.

Type 3 motra are buildings whose appearance is traditional but whose basic structure is not, such as stores and restaurants in the modern period that have attempted to attract customers by creating a traditional atmosphere despite their modernism.

Above: Type 1 motra, a recently constructed rural residence in Fukui Prefecture built in the modern period but traditional in both construction techniques and appearance. Spaces between the exposed posts are filled with bamboo or wood lattice covered inside and out with mud mixed with straw and plastered white.

Above left: Type 1 motra, a teahouse (Nara Park, Nara City) built in the modern period, with a traditional structure and thatched roof.

Below: Meiji Period buildings tended toward the baroque in terms of surface decoration, exemplified in this detail from a wooden Japan Red Cross Society hospital constructed in Tokyo in 1877 and rebuilt in Meiji Mura in 1974.

Pseudo-Western and Blended Styles

Above: Pseudo-Western style. Detail from a police box constructed in front of Tokyo Train Station, completed in 1914. The station itself was constructed of a steel frame with red brick and white stone. The police box, however, was of reinforced concrete faced with ceramic tiles that resembled the station's brick masonry. The use of exterior wall tiles, often made of heat- and cold-resistant porcelain, is used in Japan even today to conceal the underlying structure.

Many of the early buildings constructed after the Meiji Restoration were designed by Western architects in a variety of foreign styles. There were also a number of "pseudo-Western" structures that involved Japanese interpretations of foreign styles. Eventually, Japanese architects mastered Western techniques and styles and went on to create buildings that successfully "blended" traditional and Western elements.

Pseudo-Western Architecture

From the end of the Edo Period to the early Meiji Period, many government buildings, private businesses, and factories were constructed in stone and brick. Because the Japanese lacked experience with such materials, these new structures were built by foreign architects or Japanese carpenters under the guidance of foreigners. After learning about Western style architecture on the job, or studying Western style structures, many of these Japanese carpenters accepted contracts on their own, frequently in rural areas. The resulting "pseudo-Western" style buildings typically combined Western designs with traditional Japanese elements. An early example was the Tsukiji Hotel, built in Tokyo in 1868 by Shimizu Kisuke, based on plans drawn up by the American architect Richard P. Bridges. The well-known Tsukuji Hotel, which burned several years after it was built, was an eclectic wooden building with a tower, crisscross lathe and plaster walls, and a hipped roof with a weathercock.

Right: Stone lithograph by Motoharu of the Ministry of Finance, Tokyo, a pseudo-Western style building.

The Education Order of 1872 encouraged Western learning. Within a short period of time, pseudo-Western style schools had spread all over Japan. Most of these schools were simple rectangular structures with a vestibule in the center, a small tower for a clock or drum in the middle of the roof, and wood siding. Pseudo-Western style architecture continued to be built during the Taisho and Showa Periods, and even later.

Designs by Japanese Architects

Not wishing to rely permanently upon foreign expertise, the government established professional schools, such as the Imperial College of Engineering. The goal was to produce indigenous architects who could assist in defining a national identity by designing Western style buildings for government, commerce, and industry. It was not long until Japan's new architecture and engineering programs began graduating their own students. Two of the early students of Josiah Conder, professor at the Imperial College of Engineering, were Katayama Tokuma (1853–1917) and Tatsuno Kingo (1854–1919). This new breed of Japanese architects used stone in the most important buildings, such as the Akasaka Detached Palace, which was designed as the residence for the Crown Prince by Katayama. Less important buildings, such as Tokyo Station, designed by Tatsuno, were generally constructed of red bricks with steel or timber frames. The least important buildings were timber-framed weatherboard structures, favored by government ministries because they were cheaper and easier to build than stone or brick.

Blended Styles

The beginning of the 1880s saw a public reaction against the rush toward Westernization, resulting in the reassessment of indigenous techniques and styles in a more favorable light. By the 1930s, rising nationalism and militarism led to a demand that major public buildings should express Japanese sensibilities. For example, when the Imperial Museum, designed by Josiah Conder, was destroyed in the Great Kanto Earthquake of 1923, a competition was held to select an architect to design its replacement. The jury chose a design by Watanabe Hitoshi (1887–1973), who created the prototype of what became known as the Imperial Crown style, in which massive tiled roofs and Japanese decorative motifs were added to

heavy, symmetrical Western style facades. After World War II, this attempt at reconciliation was continued, with better results, under internationally trained architects such as Tange Kenzō (1913–), who strove to combine traditional elements with technological advances.

A pre-World War II example of "blended architecture" is provided by the Japan Railways Nara Station, built in 1934 and designed by Shibata Shirō and Masuda Seiichi to replace a wooden building. The building has a wooden roof with a temple-style spire that was placed on a rectangular concrete building. Both traditional and modern elements were used inside and out to create a structure that is surprisingly pleasing in design.

Maturation of Japanese Architecture

The above categories are somewhat arbitrary and should not be cast in stone. The basic point is that Japanese architecture went through a maturation process after the introduction of Western styles. The earliest Japanese builders of Western style structures were carpenters who often worked under foreign architects initially. They made various adaptations in terms of materials and techniques, but the designs remained basically Western. Eventually, a new generation of indigenous architects had the necessary skills to design Western style buildings that went beyond imitation to the creation of mature forms that proclaimed that Japan was ready to compete with Europe and the United States on the architectural scene. Some architects went even further to design new "blended" forms that were neither strictly Western nor Japanese, but original syntheses. Today, many Japanese architects continue to take their inspiration from both Western and Eastern traditions and are winning an international reputation as a consequence.

This maturation process is not new. With the introduction of continental architecture in the sixth and seventh centuries, Japanese builders mastered new forms and techniques and went on to create unique Japanese masterpieces such as Katsura Detached Palace.

Residential Architecture in the Traditional Style

Motra residences, traditional in both construction and appearance, are the result of a long history in which new elements were added and old elements were modified to create a style characterized by simple elegance and an "openness" to the outside garden. Motra residences were common prior to World War II and are sometimes constructed even today, though their popularity is declining.

Historical Background

What are commonly known as "traditional houses" are descendants of the Shoin and Sukiya styles that were developed by the aristocracy in classical and feudal times and adapted for wealthy urbanites in the Edo Period. In addition to the aristocratic *shoin–sukiya* tradition, there were also farmhouses (*minka*) and townhouses (*machiya*). But by the latter part of the Edo Period, wealthy families, regardless of their occupation and whether they lived in cities, towns, or villages, dwelt in houses that incorporated a scaled-down version of many features typical of the aristocratic tradition.

Traditional style houses continued to be built in the Early Modern Period and are sometimes constructed even today. As discussed above, motra buildings can be traditional in both structure and appearance (Type 1), traditional in structure only (Type 2), or traditional in appearance only (Type 3). The first of these types was most typical of houses in the Early Modern Period and will be described below. Despite their traditional structure and appearance, Type 1 motra residences are, of course,

not really faithful copies of their Edo Period ancestors since they make minor changes to accommodate the technological advances of the period in which they are built.

Basic Characteristics

Motra houses typically have a wooden post-and-beam frame structure that supports the roof. Vertical members of the structure rest on foundation stones, and the areas between the posts are occupied with sliding doors or latticework made of strips of bamboo or wood that are woven together and tied with straw or linen. Two layers of clay are applied on each side of the mesh and then coated with *shikkui*, a plaster made of lime, straw or sand, glue, and water, to which color is sometimes added.

The roof can be protected with a variety of materials – thatch, *hinoki* bark shingles, bamboo, or slate – but is usually covered with tiles, due in part to regulations designed to make crowded urban areas less susceptible to fire. Peripheral areas (*hisashi*) have their own roofs.

Exterior window and door openings are covered with panels that slide on adjacent tracks. The outside track consists of wood panels that can be closed to lock the house or to provide protection against severe weather; the next two tracks (optional) consist of sliding glass and screened panels; and the inside track consists of wooden frames covered with translucent rice paper (*shōji*) that admit the light. Interior sliding doors (*fusuma*) are made of wooden frames covered with heavy paper, often painted or stenciled with natural scenes, people, birds, animals, or abstract designs. *Fusuma* can be removed to create large interior spaces for special functions. Sometimes there are louvered transoms or decorative carved grills (*ramma*) over the *fusuma* to allow air circulation when interior doors are closed. There are usually some permanent partitions.

Traditional style houses make extensive use of elevated verandas (*engawa*), which provide a transition between the interior and the surrounding garden. Deep eaves protect the verandas from rain and keep out the summer sun, while allowing doors to be left open even when it is raining. Bamboo curtains can be lowered over window and door openings to block the sun while still providing ventilation.

The formal entrance (*genkan*) consists of sliding doors, inside of which is a ground-level area for leaving shoes and umbrellas. Beyond is a raised enclosure that provides access to interior rooms. The *genkan* is considered

Below: Exterior of the rented single-story home of Natsume Sōseki (1867–1916), one of Japan's most famous writers. Originally constructed in Tokyo around 1887 (Meiji Period), the building is a typical city motra residence with an elevated post-and-beam structure, tiled roofs, veranda, sliding doors, and kitchen at one end.

Construction Techniques

Traditional architecture in Japan employs the post-and-beam method of construction in which the roof is supported by beams that rest on posts rather than on the walls. Buildings such as shrines and temples usually employed heavy timbers whereas motra style houses generally use squared dimension lumber. This drawing illustrates horizontal beams resting on posts that extend from the bottom of the building to the roof. To these horizontal beams are attached vertical posts of varying lengths to which are fastened horizontal rafter supports (*moya*), including the ridgepole. Finally, rafters are attached to these *moya* to create a sloping roof.

Far left: Detail of a traditional frame structure showing how timbers are joined as well as how the lattice is attached.

Center and right: Constructing a suspended ceiling. Ceiling rafters are supported temporarily by a beam and rope. Ceiling boards are attached to the rafters, after which the vertical ceiling supports are attached to overhead beams.

Left: Interior of the Sōseki house. Typical motra features include *tatami* mats, a *tokonoma* bordered by a natural peeled pole, sliding doors (*shōji* and *fusuma*), and the use of natural materials and muted colors. The house is now located at Meiji Mura.

Right: Beds (*futon*) laid out on *tatami* mats for the night. Sliding *shōji* and *tokonoma* can be seen in the back.

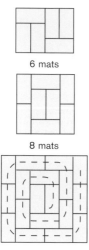

6 mats

8 mats

18 mats

Above: Typical arrangement of *tatami* mats for different sized rooms.

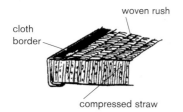

woven rush

cloth border

compressed straw

Above: Construction of a *tatami* mat.

Above: A traditional downspout consists of small linked metal cups. As a cup overflows, water is passed down the chain to the next cup, to form an interesting and dynamic pattern.

public in that visitors can enter this area without knocking or ringing the doorbell.

The *tokonoma* is a recessed alcove that has a raised floor covered with a *tatami* mat or wood. It contains an art object or flower arrangement and a hanging scroll appropriate to the season. Next to the *tokonoma* is a second alcove separated by a thin partition. This second alcove is usually a *tokowaki*, which consists of a small cupboard with sliding doors at the bottom, one or two shelves in the middle, and an additional cupboard on top. Sometimes the *tokowaki* is replaced by an *oshiire* – a large cupboard with sliding doors used for storing bedding or other household items such as cushions.

The bath and the toilet are in separate rooms and often at opposite ends of the veranda, to symbolize the difference between purification and elimination functions. Both the bath and the toilet have their own slippers, which are not to be worn in other areas. The traditional toilet was a "squat" type, which consisted of a hole above a retaining tank. Eventually, holding tanks gave way to sewage systems and flush toilets, either squat or Western style. The kitchen, often located at one side or corner of the house to form an L shape, generally has its own roof.

In contrast to farmhouses (*minka*) and townhouses (*machiya*), which usually had work areas with dirt floors, the floors of motra houses are raised wooden frames covered with *tatami* mats or a combination of *tatami* mats and boards. The size of a room is determined by the number of *tatami* mats a room contains, usually four and a half to twelve, with six being the norm. *Tatami* mats come in two sizes but are generally about one by two meters and consist of a straw foundation over which is fastened a finely woven reed mat. Around the edges are sewn cloth borders, usually black but often in other colors as well. The number of mats in a room determines the dimensions of the lumber used in the room, according to a system known as *kiwarijutsu* that was developed in earlier periods to ensure pleasing proportions and to promote standardization of parts.

Ceilings can be made of different materials. One of the most common types consists of wide thin boards, with interesting grain patterns, resting on a framework that is suspended from above. Access to upper floors is by ladders or open stairs, sometimes with drawers underneath, to make the best use of space.

Surroundings

The space around a traditional house is as important as the interior. Privacy is provided by a fence or wall that surrounds the property. Entry is through a gate, which can be relatively modest or a substantial structure with a roof, depending upon the wealth and status of the owner. The passageway from the gate to the main entrance of the house is where inhabitants switch from a public to a private mode in the sense of preparing themselves psychologically for returning to a refuge from the stress and distractions of the outside world. The basic ingredients for this passageway are water, rocks, trees, shrubs, stone lanterns, and a path.

The secret of encouraging one to focus on the immediate surroundings is to provide an interesting environment in a limited amount of space. There are a number of ways of doing this. For example, a curved path provides a greater feeling of distance than a straight path, and irregular stepping stones are more interesting than a graveled or paved walkway. Other examples of sensual stimuli are colored carp swimming in a pond, or water dripping into a stone basin from a natural bamboo pipe.

The garden is distinct from the entry passageway. Ideally, it is located so that it can be viewed from one or more of the most important areas of the house, such as a guest room where visitors are entertained and where they may spend the night. In addition to providing a visually pleasing space, one of the basic functions of a garden is to create and maintain contact with nature. The garden should be designed in such a way that it takes on a different appearance with the coming of each new season – featuring greenery in the summer, colored leaves in the fall, snow on lanterns in the winter, and flowers in the spring.

Far left: Traditional *genkan* (formal entry). Visitors leave their shoes at the first level and step up to an enclosed area that provides access to the interior of the house.

Left: Multiple tracks for sliding doors on a motra house. The doors not in use are stored in a recess at one end of the tracks.

Left below: The graveled area under the eaves is important for houses that do not have gutters and downspouts because it helps reduce splashing.

Below: Traditional style house in Kyoto with latticed doors and windows, protected by a tiled overhang.

Inns in the Traditional Style

Right: Woodblock print by Hiroshige depicting an inn in Shimosuwa, a popular post town in the Edo Period. The men in the large room have already had their baths and are being served a simple meal. In the smaller room, a man is bathing in a large wooden barrel.

Below left: Interior of Tanabe Ryokan, showing a "conversation room" where guests can relax and have tea prepared with hot water kept in a teapot hanging over the fire. The room has elements of a traditional Shoin style room, such as the built-in desk.

Below right: Exterior of Tanabe Ryokan in Takayama City. The building is typical of the region, with latticed windows and sliding doors. This style of architecture was originally brought from Kyoto by those escaping the clan wars at the end of the Heian Period.

The first inn in Japan is said to have been built in the eighth century for traveling priests. In the Edo Period, pilgrims stayed at inns associated with famous temples and shrines, and *daimyo* stopped at post town inns on their way to and from Edo. In the Modern Period, new style inns have evolved to meet the needs of travelers.

Ryokan

Traditional inns do not have a unique style of architecture since any large house could be turned into an inn. *Machiya* were especially easy to adapt for use as inns because they had interior halls on which the rooms faced, in contrast to the more typical residential arrangement in which rooms were separated only by sliding doors. Some of the finest traditional inns today were formerly the *machiya* homes of wealthy businessmen in cities such as Kyoto. An inn that is traditional in both structure and appearance, either because it has survived from earlier times or has been constructed in the traditional way (Type 1 motra), is known as a *ryokan*.

Ryokan are often small wooden structures with one or two floors, but some are large with several wings. After entering the *genkan* through sliding doors, guests leave their shoes at ground level and step up to the lobby where they are provided with slippers, meet the owner or manager, and register. They are then taken down a hall to their rooms, each with

its own name, such as a tree or flower. Rooms are in the residential style, with *tatami* mats, a *tokonoma* containing a seasonal flower arrangement and hanging scroll, an adjacent alcove with decorative shelves, and large cupboards fronted by sliding doors where the bedding is kept. A sophisticated *sukiya* atmosphere is provided by techniques such as leaving the bark on the pole at the corner of the *tokonoma*, allowing the straw to show in the plastered walls, and using wide boards with an interesting grain in the suspended ceiling.

The only furnishings in prewar *ryokan* were a low table and several cushions (*zabuton*), sometimes with a hole under the table for one's feet, as well as for a container with hot charcoal, one of the few sources of heat in the winter. When the charcoal was in use, the table was covered with a heavy *futon* that reached the floor to keep in the heat, and a wooden cover was placed on the *futon* to provide a hard surface for eating or writing. Eventually, these traditional *kotatsu* gave way to a table with an electric heating element fastened to its undersurface. Today, inns are equipped with modern air-conditioning units that heat in the winter and cool in the summer. Another recent modification is the addition

of a small sitting area between the *tatami* mat room and the exterior windows, equipped with Western style chairs and a table. Sliding doors separate the sleeping and sitting areas, and sliding doors or windows open on gardens or natural scenery. Other popular postwar additions are a television that sits in the *tokonoma* and a small refrigerator in the *genkan* where cold beer, pop, and snacks are kept.

Bath and Meals

After guests have left their slippers in the entrance to their private room and are seated at the low table, the hostess explains the layout of the inn and provides information on meal times and when the bath is open. She prepares green tea to accompany the sweets to be found on the table and then leaves so that guests can relax.

Some time before dinner, guests shed their street clothes, don the informal kimonos (*yukata*) provided by the inn, and make their way to the bath area, which is usually segregated by sex. The bath consists of an area where clothes are left in a basket and where one dries after the bath, and the bathing area where one scrubs with soap and water before entering a tub or pool, made of wood or ceramic tiles, large enough to hold several people. Some inns also have an outdoor bath (*rotenburo*) where one can sit in the steaming hot water and enjoy the surrounding greenery. Often the hot water has a high mineral content, supplied by natural hot springs with different therapeutic qualities. Following the bath, a multi-course dinner is served in the room, after which guests go for a stroll in their *yukata* while the maid replaces the table with the bedding, which is laid out on the *tatami*.

Ryokan Hotels

After World War II, Japan made a fast economic recovery and the newly affluent population began to travel, usually in groups. For example, companies often chartered large buses to take their employees to hot spring resorts – to relieve stress and enhance group solidarity, thereby improving productivity. To meet this demand, inns increased in size and provided party rooms for banquets and group entertainment.

Ryokan hotels are generally built of reinforced concrete and thus differ from traditional *ryokan* in both structure and appearance. The lobby is usually carpeted, the hot baths are sometimes enormous (12–15 meters in

Left: Country inn from the Edo Period in Rikuzen, Iwate Prefecture. The thatched roof has a smoke vent on the right. The supplemental roof over the entrance is made of boards and weighted with stones.

length), and there are special areas with facilities such as arcade games, massage chairs, and pop and cigarette machines. Guest rooms are often indistinguishable from those of traditional *ryokan*, and the food and service can be equally as good.

Below: Yufuin Onsen Hotel, a Japanese hot spring resort in Kyushu. Traditional décor, including a translucent sliding door (*shōji*), is combined with a Western style bed.

Left: Lobby of Yūzansō, a *ryokan* hotel in Ogoto Onsen, Shiga Prefecture. Seen in this photograph are a large lobby, souvenir shop, and coffee shop. The hotel has 121 guest rooms, banquet rooms, a large convention hall, and several entertainment and sports facilities, including a bowling alley.

Temples and Shrines in the Traditional Style

Much of Tokyo was destroyed by earthquake, fire, and war. As a consequence, very few Edo Period buildings have survived. Most temples and shrines are motra structures, meaning they have been built in the Modern Period but in a traditional style. Sometimes they are traditional in both structure and appearance, whereas in other cases new materials and techniques have been combined with traditional designs.

Meiji Shrine

Meiji Shrine was dedicated to the Emperor Meiji (1852–1912), known as the "Father of Modern Japan" for his role in opening Japan to the outside world, and to his wife, Empress Shōken. Set in a large compound wooded with over 100,000 trees donated from all parts of the country, this imperial shrine, designed by the architect Ito Chūta (1867–1954), is one of the most impressive in Japan. Built in 1920 with State funds, Meiji Jingū was destroyed in a 1945 air raid but rebuilt with private donations in 1958 in the traditional style. A *torii* constructed of 1,500-year-old Taiwanese cypress trees, one of the largest in Japan, dominates the approach. It is 12 meters high and spans 9.1 meters from post to post. The Main Shrine, built in an unadorned Nagare style, consists of the Honden (Main Hall) and the Haiden (Worshipper's Hall). The materials are mainly Japanese cypress with copper plates for the roofs.

Other important buildings are the Shinko (Treasure House), a concrete building constructed in the Azekura (log storehouse) style of the Shōsōin Repository in Nara; the Shiseikan (Hall for the Martial Arts),

a modern building constructed in 1973; and the Kaguraden (Hall of Shinto Music and Dance), constructed in 1993 in the traditional Nagare shrine style.

The Gyoen (or Naien) is a park dedicated to the empress. Originally the gardens of the Edo residences of two *daimyo* families, the park is situated between the *torii* entrance and the Main Shrine. Considered to be one of the best in Japan, it is home to around 365 different species of trees, as well as around 100 varieties of irises. On New Year's day, more than three million worshippers visit the shrine to pray for longevity and prosperity in the new year.

Zōjōji Temple

Founded in 1393, Zōjōji is a chief temple of the Jōdo sect of Buddhism. It is dedicated to Jizō, the patron saint of travelers and departed children. Selected by Tokugawa Ieyasu as a mortuary temple in 1590, Ieyasu's son Hidetada and six later shoguns are buried in its ornate mausoleums. The Sanmon (Main Gate), constructed in 1605 in the Chinese Tang style, is a rare example of early Edo Period architecture. All of the other buildings on the grounds were destroyed in World War II. The main building is a 1974 reconstruction. In the garden are two trees – one planted in 1879 by General Grant, the 18th President of the United States, and the other, in 1982, by President George Bush Sr.

Yasukuni Shrine

Yasukuni Jinja has been the topic of great controversy in Japan since the end of World War II. It is home to the souls of more than 2.5 million Japanese war dead, including 14 convicted Class A war criminals. The original name of the shrine was Shōkonsha, meaning "the shrine for inviting the spirits." Established

Above: Crest on a heavy wooden door at Meiji Shrine.

Above right: The Haiden (Worshipper's Hall) at Meiji Shrine.

Below: The Sanmon Gate at Zōjōji Temple, in the Chinese Tang style, is a rare example of early Edo Period architecture.

in 1869, the main building is an imposing Shimmei structure (entrance on the long side) with an enormous 15-meter bronze *torii* at the front, constructed in 1887. Situated on the grounds is Japan's only public modern military museum, which opened in 1872.

Sengakuji Temple

On a low bluff overlooking Tokyo Bay is one of Edo's most famous landmarks – the graves of the 47 *rōnin* (masterless samurai), located at the small temple of Sengakuji. The story of their loyalty and heroism is the subject of many stories, films, and plays, including the famous Kabuki play *Chūshingura*.

Sengakuji is a Sōtō Zen temple originally built by Tokugawa Ieyasu near Edo Castle. In the Edo Period, the Sanmon (Main Gate) was one of the three most famous gates in the city. After a disastrous fire, the temple was moved to its present location in the eighteenth century. The Main Hall was destroyed by bombs in 1945 and rebuilt in the Kamakura Zen style in 1953.

Sensōji Temple

Legend says that in the year 628, two brothers fished a statue of Kannon, the goddess of mercy, out of the Sumida River, and even though they put the statue back in the river, it always returned to them. Consequently, Sensōji, commonly known as Asakusa Kannon Temple, was built in 645 to enshrine the tiny golden image, making it Tokyo's oldest temple. During the Edo Period, Sensōji, crowded with hawkers and entertainers, was a popular stop on the way to the nearby Yoshiwara "floating world" district. Its popularity increased in the 1840s when the shogun banished Kabuki theater to the Asakusa district. Most of the present buildings at Sensoji are postwar concrete reconstructions in the traditional style, with tiled roofs.

The most famous structure at Sensōji Temple is the Kaminarimon (Thunder Gate), depicted in woodblock prints. The gate burned in 1865 and was rebuilt in 1955. Located at the beginning of a long row of shops that leads to the temple compound, Kaminarimon Gate houses statues of guardian deities, Fūjin and Raijin, the gods of wind and thunder.

Asakusa Shrine

Situated on the grounds of Sensōji Temple is Asakusa Shrine, dedicated to the brothers who netted the Kannon image. This original building, founded in the mid-seventeenth century by the shogun Tokugawa Iemitsu, miraculously escaped fire and wartime destruction. It is designated an Important Cultural Property. The main building is a fine example of the elaborate Gongen style, popular in the Edo Period. Like the shrines at Nikkō, Gongen buildings enshrine deified human beings.

More popularly known as Sanja-sama, "shrine of the three guardians," Asakusa is the focus of the Sanja Matsuri, one of Tokyo's largest festivals which takes place every year on the third weekend in May. The climax comes on the second day when hundreds of people carry over 100 *mikoshi* (portable shrines), each weighing around 1000 kilograms, through the streets near the shrine.

Top: The main building at the small Sengakuji Temple, destroyed in 1945, was rebuilt in the Kamakura Zen style.

Above: Bell Tower at Sengakuji Temple.

Left: The Shimmei style Main Hall at Yasukuni Shrine was constructed in 1869.

Sensōji Temple

When approaching Sensōji Temple from the south, visitors pass through the outer gate, the Kaminarimon, or Thunder Gate, an impressive red-lacquered structure named for its two guardian deities of thunder and wind (Raijin and Fūjin). Hanging in the portal of the gate is a large paper lantern – one of the most famous sights in Tokyo. A 200-meter street, the Nakamise, which is flanked by numerous small souvenir and food shops, leads from the Kaminarimon to the temple's main gate, the Hōzōmon, a two-story structure that houses fourteenth-century Chinese sutras on the upper floor. The large straw sandals of the Hōzōmon's two protective deities are hung on the gate's rear wall. Beyond the Hōzōmon and in front of the Main Hall is a large bronze bowl where visitors leave lighted sticks of incense. The buildings in the main compound were repeatedly destroyed by fire and other calamities since their beginnings in the seventh century, most recently in 1945. Reconstruction of the Main Hall was completed in 1958, the pagoda in 1973, and the Yagodō and Awashimadō Halls as recently as 1994.

Yagodō Hall houses recent Buddhist statues.

Awashimadō Hall is dedicated to a deity that takes care of women.

Dembōin, the living quarters of the Abbot of the temple.

Detail of the pagoda, showing the complex bracketing system.

The five-story pagoda was built in 1973 after the original, constructed by Tokugawa Iemitsu, was destroyed in 1945. At slightly over 53 meters, it is the second highest pagoda in Japan, superceded only by Tōji Temple in Kyoto.

Nakamisedōri, a street leading from the main entrance to the temple compound, is lined with small shops selling traditional crafts and food.

Kaminarimon Gate houses statues of the guardian deities Fūjin (god of wind) and Raijin (god of thunder).

The original Hōzōmon Gate was destroyed by fire in 1631, rebuilt by Tokugawa Iemitsu in 1636, and destroyed again in 1945. The present two-story concrete structure dates to 1964. Priceless sutras are stored on the upper floor.

The concrete Main Hall, completed in 1958, houses a group of large votive paintings donated in the eighteenth and nineteenth centuries by some of Edo's leading artists. The small golden image of Kannon reputedly rescued from the Sumida River in 628 is hidden from view.

Enormous paper lanterns hanging in the Main Hall were donated by local geisha associations.

The ornate Asakusa Shrine, constructed in 1649 in the Gongen style, is dedicated to the two brothers who rescued the Kannon image from the river, as well as to their lord.

Sensōj's eastern entrance is guarded by Nitenmon Gate, the oldest structure on the grounds. Originally built in 1618, it survived the 1945 air raids. It is all that remains of a shrine honoring Tokugawa Ieyasu. It was relocated to its current location in 1651.

Modern Architecture

Japan is an old, traditional society. At the same time, it is a modern society that experienced rapid industrialization and urbanization in the Meiji Period and again in the period following World War II. Today, faced with crowding and high land prices, Japan is experimenting with new ways to provide safe and comfortable living and working environments for its people.

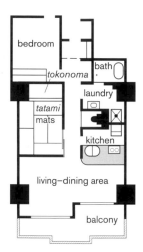

Above: Typical room arrangement for a 2LDK apartment.

Opposite: A growing number of affluent Japanese live in custom-designed homes that combine traditional features, such as a post-and-beam structure with exposed ceilings, with modern furniture.

Below left and right: Show home by Sumitomo Ringyō Company that combines traditional and modern features.

Residential Architecture

In Early Modern Japan, the majority of Japanese people lived in rural areas, either in a farm village or on their own plot of land. In either case, rural houses (*minka* or motra) were often quite spacious as the ideal was to have an extended family in which the eldest son continued to live with his parents after he got married. The process of urbanization, which had begun much earlier, continued, however, as people moved to the large cities to find work and an easier way of life. Though many people returned briefly to the countryside during and immediately after World War II, to find food and escape the massive destruction of Japanese cities, the process of urbanization soon recovered as Japan rapidly rebuilt its industrial infrastructure and continued to modernize. Today, the majority of Japanese live in urban areas where owning a private home is extremely expensive. As a consequence, the most common residential layout is called "2LDK," meaning a living–dining area plus two bedrooms, one for the parents and one for the children. In other words, the

average Japanese family today is a nuclear rather than an extended family. Grandparents usually have to fend for themselves as there is no room for them to live with their children.

Most of those who cannot afford to own a private home live in high-density apartment blocks known as *danchi*, which are built wherever land becomes available. Some *danchi* are like small cities with hundreds of buildings and thousands of tenants.

In general, the quality of postwar houses, especially in urban areas, was quite poor. Buildings were constructed as cheaply as possible, often of concrete. A certain degree of "shabbiness" was accepted, and even valued in traditional Japan, due to aesthetic values such as *wabi* and *sabi*, which emphasized the beauty of poverty. The shabbiness associated with poorly constructed concrete buildings, however, produced a much different effect. Gradually, these postwar buildings are being torn down and replaced with modern structures that recapture some of the elegance, simplicity, and attention to detail of traditional residential architecture.

Above: Atrium in the Diamor Underground Shopping Center. Natural light, unusually high ceilings, and wide passageways dispel the notion that underground areas are dark and confined. On either side of the passage are entrances to trendy fashion boutiques. This passage exemplifies the generous use of space in the public passageway.

Above: Important to the success of underground shopping areas is the ability to provide an attractive and visually stimulating environment. This is accomplished by the generous use of statues, art displays, and decorative techniques such as those shown here.

Underground Architecture

Population congestion and the high cost of land in urban areas have other consequences as well. At one time, buildings were limited to three or four stories because of the dangers of earthquakes and typhoons. Modern engineering and construction techniques, however, allow the use of modern skyscrapers. Another space-saving technique is to go underground. Japan has the largest number of sub-surface shopping and commuting areas in the world. Shopping arcades are also very popular because they combine a concentration of small businesses with a covered walkway that allows people to shop while walking to and from work or other destinations. Elevated highways provide space for a type of shopping arcade underneath, space not suitable for residential buildings or offices.

The original purpose of underground development in Japan was to provide pathways that would separate pedestrians and vehicles, thereby ensuring the greater safety of those on foot and reducing above-ground congestion. Underground passages were mainly constructed beneath public areas, such as existing streets and parks. Rail and subway lines were built under these passages. The two underground levels were connected so pedestrians could access the public transportation system. Gradually, these underground areas were extended to include shopping plazas and many other facilities.

In 1974, the national government issued a document called "Basic Policies on Underground Shopping Malls." It stipulated that an underground shopping complex should contain parking lots, underground walks, shops, offices, and other facilities for providing services and recreation; be constructed under public spaces such as roads, and be located near a railway station. By the end of 1995, there were 79 such complexes in Japan, eight of which were located in Osaka.

Underneath Osaka is a vast system of commercial complexes and pedestrian highways that link the numerous private rail and subway lines, as well as multi-level car parks and the lower levels of numerous business and government buildings. Upon reaching one of the many entrances to this underground network, the commuter can shop, take part in

recreational activities, eat, bank, visit a doctor, book a trip with a travel agent, or travel to work without ever coming to the surface. Of the more than three million people who use this system daily, not all are commuters. Many people have come to prefer the visually stimulating underground world to the crowded and sometimes dangerous outside environment. European style "sidewalk" cafes and countless restaurants offering international cuisines are especially popular.

In addition to the main pedestrian traffic walks constructed under public streets and parks, auxiliary traffic lines have been provided under or through the basement areas of private buildings. In the Diamor section of the complex, public passageways are broad and brightly illuminated. The entire underground area is divided into eight-block sections sepa-rated by shutters to prevent the spread of fire and smoke. There are also lamps and buzzers to assist in the safe escape of the handicapped. An Information Management Center monitors information on underground conditions in the complex and communicates with disaster prevention centers of connected buildings. The atrium area consists of a movable dome that opens automatically to function as a vent in case of fire, and fire-extinguishing equipment can be remotely operated from the Information Management Center.

Some of the advantages of underground development are improved public health due to the absence of above-ground pollution from automobiles, more efficient crime control, and the ability to provide an attractive environment that is immune to weather conditions and natural disasters.

Above: Central Square at Yebisu Garden Place in Tokyo, one of several "cities within the city." Opened to the public in 1994, it is built on the former site of the Yebisu brewery. A large array of shops, restaurants and bars, offices, residential spaces, and museums cater to the needs of locals and visitors.

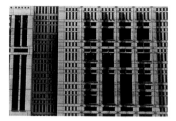

Above: Detail from Tange Kenzō's Tokyo Metropolitan Government offices, inspired by an architectural drawing of the ceiling structure of an old farmhouse in Osaka.

Below: Osaka Dome, a multi-purpose building with a retractable dome.

Civic and Business Buildings

When Tokyo, which sits on a major fault, rose from the ashes of World War II, the only major architectural constraint was the need to develop earthquake- and fire-resistant structures. The resulting experimental attitude, combined with postwar prosperity, produced an architectural diversity that provides some of the best examples of modern trends in civic and business buildings.

In response to the constant danger of earthquakes, many Japanese and foreign architects who built monuments to themselves and their clients in Japan's robust postwar economy worked primarily in reinforced concrete – a radical departure from the wood architecture of the past. Technological developments in both design and construction techniques allowed architects to experiment with new concepts in a way that was consistent with the emphasis upon individualism and self-expression that swept Japan after the war.

Because Tokyo is the center of government, business, and contemporary culture in Japan, it has attracted some of the world's best and most innovative architects, such as Tange Kenzō, Isozaki Arata, Maki Fumihiko, Kurokawa Kishō, and Andō Tadao. Most of Japan's best contemporary architects have been internationally trained and show the influence of the Swiss architect Le Corbusier and the German architect Walter Gropius.

The first skyscraper in Japan, the Kasumigaseki Building, was completed in 1968, incorporating the latest in earthquake technology. A number of other skyscrapers were built soon after. The Tokyo Metropolitan Government offices was the tallest building in Tokyo when it was completed in 1990. It is the brainchild of Tange Kenzō, who designed the gymnasium complex for the 1964 Tokyo Olympics – one of the most innovative buildings in the world at the time. Tange was a champion of what became known as the International Style or Modern Movement.

The main building of Tokyo Metropolitan Government offices, with its twin towers, is 48 stories high. The tops of the towers are rotated 45 degrees, giving the building a twist that breaks the symmetry and provides a feeling of dynamism. The surface is composed of glass, granite, and marble, woven into a rich and complex pattern. The twin towers are part of an enormous "post-modern" plaza constructed in the same design and with the same materials. An average of 6,000 people, mostly tourists, visit the offices each day.

Tokyo International Forum, situated in the heart of the financial district of Marunouchi, provides 144,000 square meters of cultural facilities, including museums, theaters, and art galleries. Completed in 1996, it is a modernistic combination of square buildings that reflect the traditional architecture of the surrounding area and a curved, leaf-shaped hall that follows the lines of the adjacent railway. The hall is 57 meters high, 30 meters wide, and 210 meters long. At either end are columns that support the cables and tension bars that provide the basic structure for a vast interior space with various levels of pedestrian pathways. The overall effect, with the overhead glass dome, is one of lightness and grace.

Across the street from the International Forum and adjacent to Tokyo Station, Pacific Century Place is a 31-story steel and concrete structure with a glass curtain wall. The building, completed in 2001, is the result of a joint venture by Nikken Sekkei and Takenaka Corporation. To preserve the public space around the train station, the building is raised 30 meters off the ground by four supporting concrete posts, 3.4 meters in diameter. In front is a circular structure for bringing in fresh air and on the back is a viscous core that dampens the energy of an earthquake by 15 percent. Other technological innovations include an automatic sensor that controls indoor light in accordance with the amount of sunlight.

Many other cities in Japan also have interesting examples of modern architecture. Only a few can be mentioned here. The Solar Ark, completed in Gifu City in 2002, is an enormous solar power generating plant owned by Sanyo Electric Co. Ltd – the largest of its kind

Left: Opened in 2003, Roppongi Hills, Tokyo, is another "city within the city." At the center of the redeveloped parklike city stands the 54-story Mori Tower named after the company and its president that built it. Walk-ways and gardens link residential, recreational, and office spaces.

Below: With its central tower composed of four interlocking inverted pyramids, the 1996 Tokyo International Exhibition Center (better known as Tokyo Big Site) is one of the most distinctive architectural struc-tures in the city.

1 **Sanyo Solar Ark**, in Gifu City, is the largest solar power generating plant in the world.

2 **Tokyo International Forum** is a curved, leaf-shaped hall with a vast open interior and a striking overhead glass dome.

3 **Citizens' plaza of the Tokyo Metropolitan Government offices.** The government offices are housed in the twin towers seen in the background.

4 **Akita Municipal Gymnasium** is modeled after the Olympiad in Greece.

in the world. The 315-meter-long building was designed to look like an ark embarking toward the future. The structure is supported on only four columns, giving the impression that it is floating in the air. The more than 5,000 solar modules mounted on the south wall generate approximately 530,000 kilowatt hours a year and also illuminate 77,200 red, green, and blue computer-controlled LED light panels that create a variety of astonishing visual images.

Two public facilities worthy of note are Osaka Dome and Akita Municipal Gymnasium. Osaka Dome, opened in 1997, is a multipurpose structure with a retractable dome that includes a baseball stadium, concert stages, galleries, amusement and restaurant areas, and facilities for exhibitions and meetings. It has one underground floor and nine stories above ground. The wavy form surrounding the roof is intended to resemble

clouds. Akita Municipal Gymnasium, which opened in 1994, was modeled after the Olympiad in Greece. Forty meters high, it is the largest gymnasium in the Tohoku area.

One of the most spectacular modern buildings in Japan is Umeda Sky Building in Osaka, completed in 1993. It consists of two 40-story skyscrapers connected by a "floating garden" observation deck that offers spectacular views of the city. Architect Hara Hiroshi's aim was to create a vast city in the air, composed of skyscrapers linked by escalators, footbridges, and hanging gardens. Although the present structure falls short of this dream, it has become one of Osaka's primary tourist destinations.

Contemporary buildings, such as those described above, are a vivid reminder that Japan, though rooted in the distant past, is also a modern country that is responding to the architectural needs of today's society.

Above: The twin towers of Umeda Sky Building in Osaka are connected by a "floating garden" observatory.

Glossary

Note: The long ō and ū are dropped for words commonly used in English.

amado heavy wooden doors or shutters that can be closed in inclement weather

Amida Buddha Buddha of the Western Paradise

buke yashiki samurai house

bunraku classical puppet theater

bushidō the Way of the Warrior

chanoyu tea ceremony, often referred to as *sadō*, the Way of Tea

chigi crossed finials on the roof of a Shinto shrine

chise traditional Ainu house

Daibutsuyō Great Buddha style temple architecture originally used in the Kamakura Period

Daigokuden Hall of State

daimyo lord of a castle

Dainichi Nyorai the cosmic Buddha of esoteric Buddhism

danchi high-density multi-unit apartment complex

donjon castle keep; primary structure in a castle

fusuma opaque (solid) sliding panel which run on tracks, usually covered with decorated paper

futon mattress and comforter placed on flooring that can be folded and stored during the day

gasshō steep-roofed "praying hands" style farmhouse

gejin outer area for the uninitiated in a Wayō temple (in contrast to *naijin*)

genkan entrance area or vestibule of a residence

Haiden worship hall of a Shinto shrine where devotees can enter

haniwa terracotta figurine placed on the slopes of a tomb mound

Heiankyō early capital on the site of the present-day Kyoto

heichi jūkyo flatland dwelling in which the ground served as the floor

Heijōkyō early capital on the site of the present-day Nara

hinoki Japanese cypress traditionally used for building temples

hisashi peripheral extension of a traditional building with its own roof

Hondō main hall of a Buddhist temple

Honden main hall of a Shinto shrine where the *kami* is enshrined

hottatebashira pillars sunk in the ground

irimoya hipped-and-gable roof

irori open hearth

iseki historic remains or relics

jōdan raised area for receiving guests in a formal Shoin style room

Jōdo the Pure Land or Western Paradise

kabuki classical theater originally developed for the common people

kami divine spirit or Shinto deity

Kannon Bosatsu goddess of mercy

katsuogi short poles placed across the roof ridge of a Shinto shrine

kaya reed used in thatching

ken bay or space between the pillars of a traditional building

kirizuma gable roof

kofun ancient tomb or tomb mound

Kondō another name for Hondō

kura storehouse

Kyōgen comic interlude between Noh plays

machiya merchant residence-shop usually referred to as a town house

minka house of the common people; usually referred to as a farmhouse

minshuku bed-and-breakfast establishment

mappō latter days of the Buddhist law

mon gate

monzeki temple whose head is a member of the imperial family

motra traditional style building constructed in the modern period, i.e. after 1868

moya central area of a traditional building, often surrounded by peripheral areas known as *hisashi*; the term *moya* also refers to a rafter support

naijin inner sanctum containing the altar of a Wayō temple (in contrast to *gejin*)

noh (or nō) classical theater originally developed for aristocrats

Oda Nobunaga first of the three great military leaders who unified Japan in feudal times

pagoda multi-tiered Buddhist structure derived from the Indian stupa; it originally contained a relic of the historical Buddha

ramma louvered transom or decorative carved grill above an interior sliding door

ryōbu Shinto mixing of Buddhist and Shinto beliefs, practices, and architectural forms

ryokan traditional inn

Secchūyō eclectic style temple architecture

Shaka the historical Buddha

shimenawa Shinto rope indicating a sacred space or object

shinden main building in a Heian Period élite residential complex; the *shinden* is attached to subsidiary buildings by covered halls

Shoin style originally an office that developed in the Muromachi Period into a formal room with features such as a *tokonoma*, built-in desk, and staggered shelves

shōji translucent, paper-covered sliding panel

shogun military ruler in the feudal period

Sōan teahouse small rustic teahouse ("grass hut" style)

suiboku-ga black ink painting

Sukiya style informal version of the Shoin style favored in upper-class mansions

takayuka raised floor

tatami mat straw foundation covered with a woven reed mat; roughly 1 x 2 meters

tateana jūkyo pit dwelling

tokonoma recessed alcove

torii entrance gate (without doors) to a Shinto shrine

Toyotomi Hideyoshi second of the three great military leaders who unified Japan in feudal times

Tokugawa Ieyasu third of the three great military leaders who unified Japan in feudal times; founder of the dynasty after which the Tokugawa (Edo) Period is named

uji clan

ukiyo-e woodblock print

wabi-sabi aesthetic concept that refers to the austere taste associated with the tea ceremony

Wayō Japanese style temple architecture based upon early continental styles

yamabushi mountain monks

Zenshūyō Zen style temple architecture introduced from China in the Kamakura Period

Bibliography

Alex, William, *Japanese Architecture*, New York: George Braziller, 1963.

Black, Alexandra and Noboru Murata (photographer), *The Japanese House: Architecture and Interiors*, Rutland (Vermont), Boston, and Tokyo: Tuttle Publishing, 2000.

Blaser, Werner, *Japanese Temples and Tea-Houses*, New York: F. W. Doge, 1956.

Bognar, Botond, *Contemporary Japanese Architecture: Its Development and Challenge*, New York: Van Nostrand Reinhold, 1985.

Boyd, Robin, *Japanese Architecture*, New York: St. Martin's Press, 1988.

_____, *New Directions in Japanese Architecture*, New York: George Braziller, 1980.

Brown, S. Azby, *The Genius of Japanese Carpentry: An Account of a Temple's Construction*, New York: Kodansha International, 1989.

Carver, Norman F., Jr., *Form and Space in Japanese Architecture*, 2nd edn, Kalamazoo (Maryland): Documan Press, 1993.

Coaldrake, William H., *Architecture and Authority in Japan*, Oxford: Nissan Institute and Routledge Japanese Studies Series, 1996.

_____, *The Way of the Carpenter: Tools and Japanese Architecture*, Tokyo: Weatherhill, 1991.

Drexler, Arthur, *The Architecture of Japan*, New York: Museum of Modern Art, 1955.

Engel, Heino, *Measure and Construction of the Japanese House*, Rutland (Vermont), Boston, and Tokyo: Tuttle Publishing, 2000.

Frampton, Kenneth, Keith Vincent, and Kunio Kudo, *Japanese Building Practice: From Ancient Times to the Meiji Period*, John Wiley and Sons, 1997.

Fujioka, Michio and Kazunori Tsunenari, *Japanese Residences and Gardens: A Tradition of Integration*, New York: Kodansha International, 1982.

Fukuyama, Toshio (trans. Ronald K. Jones), *Heian Temples: Byōdō-in and Chūson-ji*, New York: Weatherhill, 1976.

Futagawa, Yukio and Teiji Itoh (trans. Paul Konya), *The Essential Japanese House: Craftsmanship, Function, and Style in Town and Country*, Tokyo: Weatherhill, 1967.

_____, *The Roots of Japanese Architecture*, New York: Harper and Row, 1963.

Hashimoto, Fumio (trans. H. Mack Morton), *Architecture in the Shoin Style: Japanese Feudal Residences*, New York: Kodansha International, 1981.

Hinago, Motoo, *Japanese Castles*, New York: Kodansha International, 1986.

Hirai, Kiyoshi (trans. Jeannine Cilliota and Hiroaki Sato), *Feudal Architecture of Japan*, Tokyo: Weatherhill, 1974.

Inaba, Kazuya and Shigenobu Nakayama (trans. John Bester), *Japanese Homes and Lifestyles: An Illustrated Journey Through History*, Tokyo: Kodansha International, 2000.

Inoue, Mitsuo (trans. Hiroshi Watanabe), *Space in Japanese Architecture*, Tokyo: Weatherhill, 1985.

Itoh, Teiji (trans. Richard L. Gage), *The Classic Tradition in Japanese Architecture: Modern Versions of the Sukiya Style*, Weatherhill, New York, 1972.

_____, *Traditional Domestic Architecture of Japan*, Tokyo: Weatherhill, 1983.

_____, *Traditional Japanese Houses*, New York: Rizzoli, 1980.

Itoh, Teiji and Kiyoshi Takai (adapt. Charles S. Terry), *Kura: Design and Tradition of the Japanese Storehouse*, Seattle: Madrona, 1980.

Itoh, Teiji and Yukio Futagawa (photographer), *The Elegant Japanese House: Traditional Sukiya Architecture*, Tokyo: Weatherhill, 1990.

Katoh, Amy Sylvester and Shin Kimura, *Japan Country Living: Spirit, Tradition, Style*, Rutland (Vermont), Boston, and Tokyo: Tuttle Publishing, 2002.

Kawashima, Chūji (trans. Lynne E. Riggs), *Japan's Folk Architecture: Traditional Thatched Farmhouses*, Tokyo: Kodansha International, 2000.

Kurokawa, Kisho, *New Wave Japanese Architecture*, Hoboken, NJ: John Wiley and Sons, 1993.

Morse, Edward S., *Japanese Homes and Their Surroundings*, Tokyo: Charles E. Tuttle, 1971, reprinted 2007.

Naito, Akira and Takeshi Nishikawa (trans. Charles S. Terry), *Katsura: A Princely Retreat*, New York: Kodansha, 1977.

Nishi, Kazuo (trans. Mack Horton), *What is Japanese Architecture? A Survey of Traditional Japanese Architecture*, Tokyo: Kodansha International, 1985.

Nitschke, Gunter, *From Shinto to Andō: Studies in Architectural Anthropology in Japan*, John Wiley and Sons, 1993.

Nute, Kevin, *Place, Time and Being in Japanese Architecture*, London and New York: Routledge, 2004.

Ōkawa, Naomi (trans. Alan Woodhull and Akito Miyamoto), *Edo Architecture, Katsura and Nikkō, Volume 20, Heibonsha Survey of Japanese Art*, Tokyo: Charles E. Tuttle, 1975.

Ōoka, Minoru and Osamu Mori, *Pageant of Japanese Art: Vol. 6, Architecture and Gardens*, Tokyo: Toto Shuppan, 1957.

Paine, Robert Treat and Alexander C. Soper, *The Art and Architecture of Japan*, 3rd edn, Pelikan History of Art Series, New Haven: Yale University Press, 1992.

Richie, Donald and Alexandre Georges, *The Temples of Kyoto*, Rutland (Vermont): Charles E. Tuttle, 1995.

Soper, Alexander C., *Evolution of Buddhist Architecture in Japan*, New York: Hacker Art Books, 1978.

Stewart, David B., *The Making of Modern Japanese Architecture: 1868 to Present*, Tokyo: Kodansha International, 1989.

Tange, Kenzō, Noboru Kawazoe, and Yoshio Watanabe (photographer), *Ise: Prototype of Japanese Architecture*, Massachusetts: MIT Press, 1965.

Taut, Bruno, *Fundamentals of Japanese Architecture*, Tokyo: Kokusai Bunka Shinkōkai, 1936.

_____, *Houses and People of Japan*, Tokyo: Sanseido, 1958.

Ueda, Atsushi, *The Inner Harmony of the Japanese House*, Tokyo: Kodansha International, 1998.

Watanabe, Yasutada, *Shinto Art: Ise and Izumo Shrines*, New York: Weatherhill, 1974.

Photo Credits

Akita City page 172 (No. 4)

Ben Simmons Photography back cover, front and back end-papers, pages 4–5, 6, 31 (bottom), 63, 86–7, 159 (bottom), 161 (center), 168–9, 171, 172 (No. 3)

Keyphotos front jacket flap, pages 8–9, 17, 18, 21, 32–3, 40–1, 45, 46 (top), 47, 48–9, 52–3, 55, 58–9, 65, 67, 71, 72–3, 74, 85 (top), 88, 89 (top), 101, 104, 116–17, 120–1, 122–3, 141

Murata Noboru front cover, pages 1, 2, 13, 14, 15, 22–3, 82–3, 91, 92, 112–13, 125, 126, 128–9, 131, 135, 142–3, 146, 147, 167

Nara Bunkazai Kenkyūjo page 42 (top)

National Museum of Japanese History page 78

Okayama Yoshinori page 121 (top)

Rekishi Kaidō Promotional Council page 170 (bottom)

Rinnōji Temple at Nikkō page 138 (top left)

SANYO Electric Co. Ltd., Japan page 172 (No. 1)

Shiraoi Ainu Museum pages 36, 37

Suzuki Toshikatsu pages 162, 163, 164 (except left), 165

Luca Tettoni page 164 (left)

Michael Yamashita pages 118, 173

Acknowledgments

We are especially indebted to Kansai Gaidai University, which has supported our research in a variety of ways and to Professor Kataoka Osamu who provided us with recent findings on prehistoric architecture. Other individuals who provided special assistance are Yoshimoto Norihito, Okayama Yoshinori, and Teresa Hurst.

Institutions that were especially helpful are the Ainu Minzoku Hakubutsukan (Ainu Museum) and the Kokuritsu Rekishi Minzoku Hakubutsukan (National Museum of Japanese History). We would also like to thank the Imperial Household Agencies in Kyoto and Tokyo, the Izumi City Board of Education, the Jingū Chōkokan (the museum affiliated with Ise Jingū), the Ise Shrine Office, Murōji Temple, the Tōshōgū at Nikko, the Rekishi Kaidō Promotional Council, Akita City, SANYO Electric Co. Ltd., and the many other institutions that provided us with information and pictures.

Three books that have been of special help to us are *Nihon Kenchiku no Mikata* (How to Observe Japanese Architecture) by Miyamoto Kenji, *Shūfuku no Techō* (Restoration Notes) by Bunkazai Kenzōbutsu Hozon Gijutsu Kyōkai (Japanese Association for the Conservation of Architectural Monuments), and *Kura: Design and Tradition of the Japanese Storehouse* by Itoh Teiji (with photographs by Takai Kiyoshi).

We are indebted to Ben Simmons Photography, Keyphotos, Murata Noboru, Okayama Yoshinori, Suzuki Toshikatsu, Luca Tettoni, and Michael Yamashita for granting permission to use their work to supplement photographs taken by the authors. Finally, we are grateful for the untiring assistance of our editor, Noor Azlina Yunus.